T0194108

Rage and Resilience

A Journey through My Beloved's Battle with Cancer

SAID NEDLOUF

RAGE AND RESILIENCE
A Journey through My Beloved's Battle with Cancer

iUniverse books may be ordered through booksellers or by contacting:

iUniverse
1663 Liberty Drive
Bloomington, IN 47403
www.iuniverse.com
1-800-Authors (1-800-288-4677)

ISBN: 978-1-4759-7765-3 (sc)
ISBN: 978-1-4759-7766-0 (e)

Print information available on the last page.

iUniverse rev. date: 12/09/2015

In Loving Memory of
Mary Kathryn Fatima Ezzahra– 1964 to 2007

Dedication

*To my ex-wife Tamara who has been supportive
throughout the entire process, and who embraced
the journey with an open heart despite parting
ways; she has shown unequaled understanding while
nurturing and raising our adopted little princesses,*

Malak and Kenza.

Acknowledgments

My brother Ali in Morocco, my good disciple for years past and now my good friend.

My brother Youssef in Atlanta and the rest of my family in Morocco, whose infinite abundance of love keeps me going.

Barbara Hartley, whom Mary called her soul mate and who stood by me as a friend throughout this experience.

Rosemary McAuliffe, a sweet and faithful soul who quietly helped and never argued about anything. I love you cuz!

Mary Maynard and her husband Russell, who were there for me and for MK in times of need.

Joe Deskovitch, with the patience and spunk to tell me that the strength of a woman is unequaled by men, religious or not. I love you Aunty Jo.

Debbie Metzger, who always smiles and who sold both my houses.

Said Nedlouf

My good friends, my Tallahassee Posse: Dawn, Scott, Jeff, Claudia, Jerry, Cathy, Robert and probably others I've forgotten, but to all of them my sincere thanks.

I further wish to acknowledge many more of my friends and Mary's friends and family, without whom the journey would have been more difficult.

Table of Contents

Preface

Today, I started writing. I didn't know what to write about at first, but I felt like there was a lot on my mind, in my heart and soul. Things that would never be expressed unless written down, never would have been said aloud, or even felt. Perhaps the embedded feelings and emotions felt so special that I then had the urge to write and say what had to be said. Perhaps those feelings and emotions are never really expressed except inside my own heart and soul. These words and feelings needed an outlet, but I hadn't let them out for many reasons. Perhaps the major reason was they have to deal with my unique profile and situation. When we feel that we are different, we do not necessarily want to share our ideas and philosophies openly and honestly with people, thus we merely socialize to fit in. It is neither a lack of courage nor that the ideas lack merit or value. I think we value our discretion and privacy to a certain extent, because we feel awkward and out-of-place expressing views that some might consider unusual.

No one knows why we go through the experiences we endure and witness. Some say they are mere coincidences; they are events that we have no control over happen and that is all there is to it. Others say that they (we) are in control of our own destiny, that we choose our fate by the decisions we make, and that there is a close correlation between actions and their consequences. That we are in charge of our lives and events. Still others believe that the hidden hand of a higher power moves matter, people, events and time according to a pre-drawn plan and towards an end result, a final destiny. No matter what the force is believed to be, whether a God, super-being, or guru, it is in charge of it all, and it directs and plans all for eventualities unforeseen to the individual. According to this view, a man or woman is merely a vehicle to his or her destiny without the privilege of navigation, like an hourglass glued to a table. So, here I find myself finally writing, and the following pages will show why.

My beloved MK always encouraged me to write, but I always rejected or resisted the urge, despite knowing that I have always had a knack for it. I can express my feelings and thoughts with ease and with a certain degree of depth and poetic quality. I love to write, but have been too lazy to dedicate time to it, not to mention that I cannot make a living from it which is probably one of the reasons that I do not take the activity seriously. But my beloved MK's insistence on writing grew, so I wrote some here and there, stories about my past, my younger years in Morocco, my reflections and inner thoughts, but mostly about my recent and very interesting work experiences. Throughout the whole process, my attitude towards the subject did not budge much.

However, with the recent events and the passing of my wife, the need to write and to express my inner struggles, grief and emotions suddenly became stronger, almost necessary. There is so much I'd like to come to grips with, so many unsaid and unexpressed feelings that I felt were missing between beloved MK and I before her passing. I can no longer speak those feelings and words to her, at least not directly and in the flesh. What to do? I am not at peace or at ease with it.

A resolution was never reached. How do I get over it? How do I make peace with myself and with the spirit of my beloved? I needed to express it, talk about and put it to rest. But I do not feel close enough to anyone in particular, not even to my own mother, to talk about these feelings and inner thoughts... I need to write. So, truly, when MK was asking me to write, little did she know that I would be writing to, for, and about her. How ironic. She always felt that I had a talent and that I could write a beautiful novel, but little did she know she would be my novel. This is, in essence, her story. I hope that in a sort of cosmic, spiritual and supernatural way, the words would reach her and she can tap on my ideas, inner thoughts and feelings, as she is central to them all. I am also hopeful and confident that writing about her, and us, will cure my aching heart.

"Let them pardon and forgive. Do you not wish that Allah should forgive you?" [24:22]"

"And be patient. Indeed, Allah is with the patient." [8:46]

Part One

This story begins- for the lack of an overall and historical background- and solely tracking a chronological stream of thoughts- on November 19 of 2006. This is the date when I took the subject of writing more seriously as my beloved was getting treatment in the Bridgeport, Connecticut area. This incidentally is the time when my emotional pains were mounting, matching her physical pains, so truly, the real need for writing began now.

November 19, 2006

I find myself in the cold in the Northeast United States (Connecticut area). MK, God bless her beautiful soul, has made the journey to this land, searching for a cure to the plague of cancer that is eating at her. She is no defeatist, but a survivor and a fighter and I think she is winning it. I am standing by her to the end; no, not end, forever is a more appropriate term. Today, her struggle continues and the road to cure has taken us to the cold and difficult Northeast during the months of winter, a far cry from the warmth of our home in sunny Florida. Nonetheless, we consider this move as a blessing and an opening of the gates of mercy that will lead us to the ultimate cure and salvation. How can we do otherwise when clearly conventional medicine as expensive, boastful and advertised has failed us? Indeed, it is a complete fallacy, and a misleading and borderline malicious science that thrives on the fear of the terminally ill to charge exorbitant amounts of money for a cure that never comes, not to mention the emotional toll that it inflicts on the patient.

The proof is clear. Conventional medicine has a shameful and deceptive record in curing cancer. And what's more disconcerting is the arrogance, self-importance and total lack of real care that the doctors exhibit towards their patients. Whereas in fact, they (the medical establishment as a whole) are no more than tools for the HMO's and various drug companies, and still have a lot to learn about providing real care and a cure to the tragedy of cancer. This is also one of the many attributes of homeopathy and alternate medicine that is abundantly provided in these treatments.

MK feels so positive, so energized and so hopeful at each round of treatment. She never felt any of that with the doctors of doom and gloom in field of regular medicine.

Reminiscing.... We had just gotten married three years before, in the summer of 2003. We purchased our own house earlier that year, and she, too, had purchased a house of her own that same year. It was a year of many accomplishments, some might even say monumental accomplishments. Two houses, a wedding and a honeymoon trip to Hawaii isn't too shabby in my humble opinion.

My story with MK, however, began long before, in the wonderful and blessed fall of 1988. I met Mary at Disney World where I had been working for less than one year as part of the exchange program. I explain, Disney World as part of their EPCOT Center World Showcase, brings together people from eleven different countries as "Cast Members," to work for Disney and share their native countries' experience: indigenous foods, shopping items, and folklore. Of course, we are talking about Disney World, so this is a very lucrative endeavor in its essence. Mary was already a veteran. She and her friends from school had been working there for several years and spent most of their school breaks, including summer vacation, at Disney World. She worked at the Harvest, which is a futuristic look on how crops could be harvested in the future, with higher yields and less dependence on factors such as waters and soil. Some of the crops grew in a sort of greenhouse-like environment, without soil and barely any water. Of course, the whole thing is imaginative at best and not terribly practical. The most practical thing is that one could get rather reasonably priced food right outside the ride. To me that was the biggest attraction, since anywhere else you go inside the park, you would be paying through the nose.

Of course, Mary would have nothing to do with my advances at first. In fact, she simply ignored me the first time that I spoke to her. We were riding the bus as it transports cast members from the locker rooms to their work sites, the Moroccan restaurant for me, the Harvest showcase for Mary. That day we were returning from work and riding the same bus back to the locker rooms. I sat at the front of the bus and she sat in front of me. I said hello to her several times, but she ignored me; she had her girlfriends shielding her, which didn't set well with me. So, like any other emotional young Moroccan man, I motioned for the girls to make way for me to talk to the hot thing that was Mary. I parted the girls around her, peeked at her and said "Hello" again. I kept saying that I could see her and she could not hide from me, and that I am not quitting till she talked to me. In the end, desperate by the time, I said, "Please, just talk to me." Finally as we were leaving the bus, she stopped and returned my hello. Cha-ching! I was happy. So, I asked if she would have a beer with me right there at the nearby Mexican pavilion. She declined, but offered to do it the next day after work, as she was busy that afternoon. "No problem," I said, I was simply ecstatic to just get to talk to that gorgeous woman with the biggest and bluest eyes I had ever seen. She was a knockout, the prettiest girl I had ever seen. Her eyes were simply amazingly beautiful. That quality has never faded, even in recent, painful days.

As we sat down to drink a couple of "Dos XX" Mexican beers on that hot and humid summer day at Disney World, the chemistry was there and the flow of mystical and sensual energies was inviting. Our date was amazing! Mary could talk about anything and everything even at her young age of 22. We talked about Morocco, America, my family and hers. Love, relationships, you name it, we talked about it. More dates would come and our relationship solidified rather quickly. On a side note, I knew this woman was very special for the simple fact that she would not acquiesce to my sexual advances until a couple of months had passed. To my amazement, I stuck out and was patient. I knew that there would be something great and even more rewarding down the road. I knew that something else beyond the physical drew me to this woman. I knew I was in for a great ride and so I was patient and nothing else mattered anymore. I was thirsty and in anticipation for every date we had. The physical love and intimacy came naturally. I do not even recall how or when. I just knew that I had found a great woman, the right companion. She simply was "the one." We talked and talked forever. I think more than anything we enjoyed our discussions about faith, spirituality and love most. Those are heavy topics for our ages and interests at the time, but she was more than willing and more than capable to talk and teach me about them.

I learned so much from her in those early days, but it was just a prelude for what was to come. Mary was to become my life mentor and guide. On many occasions, she would bring me to tears as I was homesick and she knew how to tap that emotion and empathize. I found that I could confide in her about my deepest feelings, which at the time had a lot to do with me being away from home, my family and relatives. I had no problem crying to her as she was already becoming a soul mate to whom I could trust and divulge all. She was compassionate and a wonderful listener, and she was never short on words of consolation and wisdom. Even beyond that, she was also very generous with me. Oh my Lord, she spent so much money on me. She bought me nice clothes, paid for my teeth to be fixed, and took me to fine restaurants for dinner. I was in heaven. Those were definitely some of the happiest days of my life. She was simply awesome.

I love that woman much more than words here can describe. Our love feels as if were predestined by the Lord. We used to say often to one another that we surely had met in another lifetime and form. Neither of us knew it well enough to describe it, but was sure it existed. How else can one explain the fact that two people from two worlds that are so unalike could still experience a love so strong? We were so different: we had different cultures, languages, experiences, upbringings, social statuses, family statuses, values and doctrines. We were from two different ends of the spectrum. Could our meeting have been mere chance? Nonsense, I say. I truly believe there are no coincidences in life; that whatever happens, whatever encounters and connections all have a common thread, a bigger concept designed by the invisible hand of the Maker. MK also believes it, and can explain it better than I can. She explains that people are brought together not just to fall in love, which we did, but for a greater reason. People that meet each other evolve into a relationship and sometimes die together do indeed need each other, and that is why the Lord put them together. This is a powerful statement that explains the awesome genius of the Lord as the perfect matchmaker. He creates and so knows each person well: their attributes, faults, vulnerabilities, everything, and then brings that person to the one that is most compatible. Regardless of color, creed, origin or ethnicity, the two shall undoubtedly meet because they need each other, and because the Lord knows it and has it already planned and paved the way for the meeting. But just as big a part of the Maker's plan is their ultimate separation, which has been just as planned and the way to it is has been paved. No doubt, there are similar explanations in the "unrevealed[1]" faiths, like Buddhism. I am not aware of the full extent of their explanation of this phenomenon, but I still contend that it is one and the same. In the realm of our human psyche and common consciousness as designed, created and inspired by the Maker, we know that we human beings are moved by this greater force no matter how we chose to refer to it or acknowledge it. I do not understand how anyone can say that they do not believe in God, it is like contradicting existence itself.

We have been through a lot in the more-than-twenty years together. we have seen the good and the bad; enjoyed abundance but struggled as well. We were deeply involved with each other but parted ways though briefly on occasion. We were kind to each other but had less candor in rough seas. But we loved and love even more as the years go by. Through it all we came out alright. We have seen harder years and did not succumb,

---

[1] The "revealed" faiths are considered to be Judaism, Christianity and Islam.

rather we fought and won. Won the love and the ever present and deep connection we had to each.

We imagined all, best and worst. Yet, none of us could have imagined what the year 2005 had in store for us. Without exaggeration, if there is a way to describe hell on earth, it is probably what happened to MK in 2005. But she is a fighter as I mentioned earlier; she took it in full stride and decided that she was going to heal and to live. It was easier said than done. There were several stops on the way to the continuing struggle. At each stop the pain mounted, and the anguish was more devastating.

Said Nedlouf

>Hi Hon...

>I am wishing a pleasant and healthy day... thanks for your
messages on the
>yahoo acct. I love u hon…more and more everyday... Hon u have
always been
>there for me, in good or bad, sunny and cloudy days and when at
times I lost
>all hopes.. thanks for being there.. luckily, as we grow in age,
experiences
>and spirituality, these things, the matters of life, God's not so
funny
>jokes and the challenges of earthly living.. Thank God, we do
not hit the
>panic button as violently, we accept the gifts of God and smile
back and
>give them back to God to solve.. so I say hang in there babe,
there will be
>a way out... glorious, magnificent and awesome, we are
destined for the
>blessings that God loving, fearing and Good doers are entitled
to, that God
>had promised.. All the good prayers, from Mom, others, the
healers.. all,
>are there for us.. None can stop that awesome energy, certainly
not the small
>people!

January 4, 2007

Midnight.

We all wish for the New Year to bring prosperity and happiness but so far, it has not been that type of start for me. As I sit here in the dining room of the post-surgery recovery quarters at the Charles Lewis Pavilion, aisle of the ORMC, and while Youssef, my brother, is sleeping next door in room L1016, recovering from his face and head surgeries, I am on the brink of exhaustion. I need to write as the Chaplain recommended earlier. These are very odd and weird days. I just don't understand any longer. Why? The answer comes back to me, sometimes clear and strong; sometimes faint, but there is no real satisfying answer, simply suggestions that attempt to calm the soul and the mind.

I was nursing my beloved MK, who is fighting the battle of her life to survive cancer, and all of a sudden, I am caring for my brother too after an awful traffic accident. He is lucky, very lucky in fact, to have survived the ordeal and not only survived, but he is well underway for a speedy and total recovery. *Mashaa Allah, "Praise be to the Lord."*

But why did all of this have to happen in these dreadful times? It seems to be simply the luck of the draw. I am inclined to think that there is a greater design, from above, that subtly and pervasively tries to teach us. On the brink of collapse at the limits of human endurance, I believe I will be handed a parachute to make a safe landing. We are only saved by what we have learned and able teach it to others; otherwise the whole thing is a practice in futility. The Lord does that.

MK, my baby, is sleeping. She has been for the last week. The doctors say that she has one week left to live, one week left in her beautiful life. It is hard to accept but I do, I must accept it to go on. She wanted to live, to fight and overcome, but her body can no longer withstand the continuous beating from the monstrous cancer that has plagued it. She will live on, I am sure, as the beautiful spirit that she has always been, and perhaps in the Maker's great design there is more for her elsewhere. I miss her already.

I tell her that I love her and that I am with her in body, heart and spirit, and always will be. I can only imagine how traitorous the journey is the moment her life extinguishes and so it shall be. I wanted to share the journey with her but I have to stop at some point, I can only go so far before our bodies will break apart. We much go separate ways for a while before they, we, can reunite in the presence of the grace of God. I miss her dearly.

I do not know what to do anymore. I have prayed, cried and dried my tears, and then cried some more. There is no way of controlling the stream of emotions that engulf me when I see her. I live in a realm of continuous remembrance as I go in mind, or sometimes in real life, through places and instances that we have been through and shared the memories of.

I am tired. I can't stop this continuous film running in my mind at all times. I realize that all the many things we have done have ceased to be, and will never repeat again: the long walks around the lake, the ice cream while watching movies on TV, and the ritual foot massages and brushing our teeth before bed. It is horrifying to accept the idea that all that has been about her, which has touched my life all these years, will simply stop and be just memories. Sometimes these memories are happy, but more often they are painful, and then I ask myself, what is the point of it all? Why struggle to live so much and have things only to find yourself at the brink of death, unaccomplished and unfinished? But is any life really ever accomplished and finished? That question challenges me. I do not know the answer, but I'd like to think, in my faith in Allah and in the spiritual, that I can understand, with peace and resolution, that the Lord always has a reason to do things. The lesson is always positive in the end, or at least there is some sort of a salvation that will undoubtedly come forth. I miss you love.

Weeks have gone by since we first came to Bridgeport, Connecticut seeking a homeopathic route to cure cancer. The treatment, however, has done nothing but weaken my beloved MK further to total devastation. But she is the fighter that knows no defeat or submission. She continued to fight till she could no longer stand or walk or even sleep; she was wiped out of energy and force, but continued to smile and jab with everyone. She is engaged till the last breath and is doing it all her way.

By late December, MK's condition worsened. She could no longer keep up with the many pills she had to take. The homeopathic doctor kept increasing her dosage of pills to the point that she was taking more pills than food, thus becoming unable to sustain herself and losing the energy to carry on. But carry on she did, and only when her body, mind, and soul told her to quit that she did and decided to return home. At that point she was so exhausted that, at the point of total collapse, she had to be evacuated by a lifeline flight home on the eve of Christmas 2006. Once her Oncologist saw her in Orlando on December 26 the decision was made that MK would stay home under Hospice Care and quietly, and hopefully less painfully, pass on at home.

To this date, I am unable to express the amount of hurt that I felt from the news of her impending death; it was, as the doctor put it, a matter of days unbeknownst to me at that point. MK, however, knew it all along. She had a lease on her life, which will expire in January. I came home devastated and not knowing what to do. Even at this point in the struggle MK has not given up on living, and on the power of the all merciful Lord that cures, healing and salvation would come in the darkest of times, against all the odds and sciences and doctors' opinions, that she would prevail and live. Destiny, however, was already in motion, and unfortunately by then her fate had been sealed and she would meet her Maker soon enough. Maybe the Maker had wanted for her a different cure, that of healing and salvation, that lasts forever, a cessation of the earthly life and the beginning of the everlasting hereafter in the graceful and blessed gardens of Eden. And so, it was done.

> From: Mary Kathryn
>To: "Sammy Le bon"
>Subject: Re: updates
>Date: Fri, 18 Nov 2005 18:55:05 -0500
>
>HI baby,
>
>I Miss you, let me start out by telling you that it just is not the same
>with out you handsome.
>
>How are you doing??? Sleep better last night?? The Lord is
working on us
>to make us better, for him. I pleased you went to prayer today. May
>Allah bless you Honey.
I am tired and am going to bed. I keep waking up at 5am.
>
>Night night my love
>
>I am excited to see you on the 23rd. I was only concerned b/c of
all the
>heat that just happened. We have to be smart!!! I TRUST YOU!!
>
>Love Fatima EZZAHARA!

January 7, 2007

Hey Mary Barb….

Happy New Year!!!

I am spending mine right near my beloved MK…

This evening something interesting and positive happened. As I was taking MK to the bathroom, she happened to have a moment of lucidity, clarity and awareness. So we began talking, when I reminded her of what we had previously discussed, the need for both our souls to be one, making us whole. This sense of connection could only be achieved if I had her body buried in a traditional Islamic manner so that our souls and spirits might join together in the afterlife. "Do you agree with this?" I asked her in a quiet tone, "Do you consent that I put you to rest in the same way I want to be put to rest?" And do you have no problem giving up the idea of cremation?" I waited for her response as she thought. She replied, "Yes."

Aunt Joe was right outside the room when I called for her to come in. "Hon," I said. "I want you to repeat that your wish is to be buried in an Islamic way while Aunt Joe is here as a witness." She did. I continued speaking as Aunt Joe stood near, "The Lord had said in his holy book the Quran, which doesn't contradict the holy Bible, that the soul of the faithful and true believer shall go wherever he or she wants it to go; it shall go to your Father's as you die and be buried as a believer." I said. "As a Catholic, just as it is the case for me, a Muslim, a body shall be returned to the earth where it came from… ashes to ashes… there was no mention of cremation anywhere." Aunt Joe was listening intently as MK was clearly saying that she was in agreement.

I added that I wanted nothing but the best for her and the best for the two of us, that anything I do from here on is only in the purpose to make it good for her. I have shared the best and worst with each other and in my heart I have her well-being, both earthly and in the afterlife, as my highest priority, better than anyone else that she knows, including her family and her relatives. I explained that any ceremony shall be open for all to participate in, and that a Christian priest might also have a separate ceremony after the burial, and that we will have a party afterward, which we are calling a "Graduation Party."

When I spoke with Aunt Joe again outside the bathroom, I asked her what she thought. Aunt Joe said that it was all right, but I had to inform MK's mother to straighten out the expectations on her side (MK's mother). As time permits, that will be my next task.

I know deep inside that MK and I want the best for each other, and to honor each other. If it were a question of faith and closure, each one of us would want the other to be at peace and with total and complete clean conscience, especially when the matter deals with core beliefs and religion. In doing an Islamic burial, I would have honored and made our union holy and our reunion peaceful and pleasing to the Lord.

I will still have every other ceremony the family may want in addition to the Islamic burial.

Thanks for your support… most of all, I can count on it when and if I needed it at all.

-Said

P.S. Debbie was here too and mentioned something about offering a place for the burial near Jimmy since the cemetery is non-denominational. I told her I will have to think about it and get more clarification from the Mosque since I intend to do an Islamic burial. She was completely supportive and related with her own experience with Jimmy, and how the family in New York disagreed with many things about the burial. But in the end, it was her decision since she was the one who had lived with the man, suffered with him, and loved him more than anyone else. She said that my situation is the same and that I have the right to do what I feel is best for the two of us, (MK and I) since I knew fully what was near and dear to her heart. I had shared the very best and worst for the majority of her life.

I am at peace with this. I simply want to make sure that no other feuds, hassles or arguments would tarnish such a beautiful and celebrated life when it is ready to meet the Maker.

I ask for prayers, love and support… I can always use your bright and clear ideas.

Thanks again.

January 12, 2007

A minute after midnight on a Friday.

My beloved MK took her last breath and said good-bye to life on earth. Blessed was her death as she passed, hand in hand with me as I was reading the holy Qur'an for her, and reminding her of what to say when the angel descended to accompany her soul to her eternal rest. She would have known to say that she bore witness to the oneness of the Lord and that his prophet was indeed Muhammad. Luckily, for her and for me, we had been rehearsing, *i.e.* I read to her the Shahada, or the bearing witness, to make sure she dies as a faithful, enlightened human being seeking the satisfaction of the Lord. She did.

From: Mary Kathryn
> *Date: 2005/09/25 Sun AM 11:22:44 EDT*
> *To: Sammy LeBon*
> *CC: Mary Kathryn*
> *Subject: part 1*
>
> *Hi honey,*
>
> *You have a very good point. I am doing everything that I can think of, as you mentioned(wholistic, east meets west) but I feel this pressure on me.*
That I need to do something... like I am running out of time. I keep remembering when I lived at the lake cottage.. Dowling Grove. I would hear this voice tell me I only had a few years to live. Remember, I called you crying one night at 3am. My few years are here.
>
> *I think I am in a life style habit and I feel instinctively like I want to run away. I keep saying that I feel like I want to be in solitude, but that is not what I really want or need. I need to be near YOU!!!!*
>
> *You are the only one I want to be around and be in peace. This life is like a rerun on tv with the same type of stuff happening again and again. How do I get off the Merry go round? I do not know. I want a complete change. I know this is life .... but there is a different way a better way.*
> *I left town twice once to go to the beach Anna Marie island, that was good.*
The other I needed to see my Neices and nephews, Allens kids, that was good too. but In the end not what I needed.
>
> *I am sending this b/c I do not want to loose it.*

Part Two

Sunday January 14, 2007

"The day of reckoning."

My beloved MK was laid to rest forever, in peace in the place of eternal residence near the angels of God. The service was awesome, none of us had seen anything like it, neither Jews nor Gentiles, neither Christian nor Muslim, neither Buddhist or Spiritualists…even in death MK is bring people together, making the impossible a reality, bridging gaps between faiths, cultures and creeds, putting it all together. It is her signature right.

I wanted to honor the beautiful destiny that brought us together, weaved and meshed our lives in the last 20 years, something special that we made together. It appealed to both of us that our different religious backgrounds, as distant as they may be, were something that we both could find common ground in. Something that both of us are lost in, because it looks like us, yet different because it is unique, and does not resemble anything else. So I decided to have an Islamic service alongside a Christian service, honoring both MK and I.

I am Muslim and believe in the Qur'an, a sacred book of God revealed to his prophet Muhammad. Its name means "recitation," as it was meant to be recited, read to the followers. This afternoon I am listening to such a recitation, the beautiful words read by Ahmad Bin Ali Al Ajami from Saudi Arabia. His recitation is perhaps the best there is. The words, the meaning behind them, and the stories they tell are magical.

They can have spiritual influence over listeners if they have open minds, hearts, and souls.

Surely, this is how they are affecting me. I am amazed, overcome and grounded by the words. They touch me deeply. I am not the religious type at all, but I love the words of the Qur'an and they put me in a different state of mind, a state of appeasement and total calm. It is like meditation. The messages sometimes are tense and harsh in style, but the words are soothing to the soul, and, for one who is able to make the distinction, it is a true blessing. Perhaps this deserves a little more attention and a better description. The *message* is different from the beauty of the *word*. The message has been misconstrued, misunderstood by many, certainly by the marginal, vocal and extreme minority which sees the message as literal, and its literal application as a fulfillment of the word of God. They could not be farther from the truth. The word of God and his commandments were issued in specific times. They are meant to be carried out under the strictest and most specific of conditions, and the lack of that context makes them all but null and void.

As an illustration, I quote a situation that is in much discussion these recent days: the notion of Jihad or the holy struggle. When the Lord orders the faithful to fight and kill the infidels wherever and whenever they are found, the Lord also, in the same verse, says that "if the faithful cease hostilities and seek peace, then the faithful must comply with the like and cease hostilities." The Muslims should take up arms only when transgressed upon. When Muslims are expelled from their lands, their sacred places desecrated and their loved ones attacked, only then they must rise up and fight. Indeed, God, or Allah as the Muslim calls Him, has no tolerance for killing, and for the most part the message is for peace.

The Qur'an is merely a continuation of the same of message from God: the message of piety, coexistence and good works. It's that simple. But I am talking about the beautiful words and how incredible they are when I listen to them. I can forget myself just listening to or reading them. I can feel their power, and the power of God, and this is really the way I can tell their divine source and holy origin. Only then am I completely assured of God's mighty and merciful existence. One may call this faith, but I call it intuition and spiritual awareness. I feel it, I hear it, and therefore I am sure of its reality and truth. The words of God are real; there is no need to prove them. Who needs to pursue such a meaningless endeavor? God is, and God exists in his words and by them. I love them.

I know, we were not religious at all, but we were conscious of the teachings of the Lord in whatever name we call upon him, and wanted to honor the commands of the Lord as there is salvation in the hereafter. If we do so, the Lord says that if a soul goes in his blessed way, it will be free to roam and to meet that of its counterpart, that is, spouse.

I made sure that while MK was still aware and responsive that she had complete unwavering and total understanding that the way of the Lord is the most blessed way to go in order for our souls to have closure and reunite later on. So I designed the following letter that highlights, describes and makes it clear that my

MK was fully aware of the modalities of her passing, despite the wishes of some in her family who favor cremation as a way to meet the Maker. How blind and foolish such an idea; how does one expect rest and peace and bliss when the body is burned? Isn't that the essence of hell, what we are trying to avoid?

Here is the letter, as much as I can remember of it, as the words or the text were not saved. I was simply speaking from the heart, the heavy and hurtful heart, the teary and sighing soul and weakened and struggling body. I ache all over…

> *"From the earth did We create you, and into it shall We return you, and from it shall We bring you once again." Surah (Taha), Verse 55*

January 3, 2007

My Dearest Family and Friends,

First and foremost, I want to thank each of you for being here for Mary Kathryn and I over the last 18 months, and especially over the last few days. Without your help, encouragement and continual prayers this journey would have seemed much longer and darker for both of us. Please know that you have all been an integral part of Mary Kathryn's life in one way or another. She loved all and she loved deeply.

It is with love and blessings that I come forth and share the following information regarding how my beloved Mary Kathryn's final wishes for a traditional Islamic burial ceremony will be carried out assuring us a whole (united) and holy reunion in the hereafter that is in accordance with God's commandment. It is the Islamic tradition and belief that when both the husband and wife are buried in the same traditional Islamic manner it guarantees an immediate reunion of the souls in the hereafter.

In accordance with Mary Kathryn's wishes upon her entering into eternal rest and joining our Lord the following steps shall take place immediately. It is important to note that Islamic rituals call for the body of a departed one to be buried within 24 hours of death. With this in mind please be aware that time is of the essence, and not everyone will be available to participate in these rituals. There is no pressure, Mary Kathryn will understand and she knows that you are with her in spirit.

Shortly afterward I will be giving Mary Kathryn a "Graduation Party" as she often referred to it. This celebration will be open to everyone to attend and to honor her memory. Details will be forthcoming.

In the meantime, please read over the Islamic rituals that Mary Kathryn expressed she wanted me to honor and carry out on her behalf...

• *The Hospice nurse who is present will call the time of Mary Kathryn's death.*

• *The funeral home shall be notified immediately, as will the Imam at the Mosque. The funeral home will come to the house, remove her body and take it to the funeral home. A gentleman there will handle the arrangements once she is received at the funeral home.*

• *In the traditional Islamic ritual her body will be washed and cleansed by a Muslim woman. Mary Kathryn will then be wrapped in shrouds (white cloth). This ritual is carried out in private.*

• *After Mary Kathryn's body has been washed and dressed anyone who wishes may gather together (in another room to be designated at the funeral home) for prayer and supplication of any religious denomination. There is no specific person "in charge" of the prayer or supplication. In this manner anyone who may desire to come forth and share a few words of faith from their religion should do so. Please feel free to pray in silent as well. After this time of sharing the Imam will proceed with the Islamic rituals. Later in the day at the grave site there will be a second opportunity for prayer and supplication of any religious denomination.*

• *After these offerings of prayer and supplication by her family and friends Mary Kathryn will then be taken to the Mosque. A car will be provided for the immediate family to travel from the funeral home to the Mosque. It is suggested that if you would like to attend the services at the Mosque and/or the grave site that you would follow separately in your own vehicle.*

• *Once at the Mosque a Muslim Standing Prayer Service will be performed by the Imam in the courtyard. This prayer service is open to everyone, and anyone who can attend is encouraged to do so.* **Only Muslims** *may participate in this Standing Prayer Service. Non-Muslims are there only as a witness to this prayer service. This service will last only a short time.*

• *After the Standing Prayer Service Mary Kathryn will be taken to the cemetery. There will be a graveside service with the burial following immediately. This is open to everyone regardless of their religious denomination. Prayer and supplication may be offered by both Muslim and non-Muslim family and friends.*

Flowers are welcome at the grave site. Donations made also be made to The IBC Research Foundation and the American Red Cross in honor of Mary Kathryn.

Mary's body had been at the funeral home for a couple of days. The "cleansing/ cleaning" women spent the morning cleaning and then shrouding her body to get her ready for her last resting place in the ground. Her mother was granted the permission to come in and witness part of the washing ceremony, which is not done normally. She later on confined to me that what she saw in the manner and care of the two cleaning ladies handling Mary body was very touching and beautiful. The women displayed a tremendous amount of love and compassion as they were washing Mary's body to remove any visible impurities. Mind you that this was a body that was plagued with cancer, signs of which were clearly visible on the outside.

The women rolled the coffin out and I took my last look at Mary's face. She was wrapped in white shrouds; one could smell the fragrant musk and rose water emanating from her body, but what touched me most was the expression on her face. It looked to me that it was halfway between a grin and a smile. I touched her body all over as the tears rolled down my face. I kissed her lips gently while holding her hands. She was cold… I still remember that sensation. The moment was momentous yet brief. I had to be led away. I could not bear to realize that she was no longer here, nor was she mine anymore. She was gone once and for all. That was my goodbye moment. Sadness once again gripped my soul.

People trickled in, well-wishers for me and farewell-sayers for Mary, in the back of one of the rooms. I laid down on a bench and just pondered on the moment half asleep. Thoughts were racing in my head. I wanted to say something to this audience. I wanted to clarify some things and I wanted to express the deeply felt separation. I needed to say it in words louder than my tears.

The funeral house director came to me and asked if I was ready to take Mary's body to the mosque for the prayers for the deceased. By now the mourners have all settled in the funeral hall. They have looked at, but not viewed, the coffin; they also signed the book.

Mostly, they looked at a display of photos of Mary and I and our happier days. I touched the photos, I touched her face in the photos and I turned to someone who was near. I cannot recall who they were but I do remember gesturing with my hands and saying "Why?" There was no answer.

So, I told the funeral director that I wanted to say a word. He obliged and asked everyone to take a seat inside the prayer hall.

I stood behind the podium, looking at the nearly one hundred people present in the hall; some I have never seen and whom I found out later on that were friends of Mary. Some accompanied friends of mine. Some were there that none knew; maybe they were spirits?

And so I spoke these words. I cannot say for sure in what order they came out of my mouth nor can I say for sure that I was in control. They were free flowing, unchained, as if spoken through by some magical force inside.

> *The souls of two beings who live on earth and depart from it in the way that is blessed by the Lord shall ultimately meet the Maker in glory and shall meet each other and whomever they want. Thus I shall meet the soul of my beloved MK in the heavens as she had a proper and blessed burial just as did the faithful before her. The faithful that range in name and stature from Mother Mary and all the prophets and messengers that had carried the word of God from the father of them all, Abraham to Moses, Jesus and finally Mohammad... what a way to go and what an*

honor to count amongst those distinguished people.

MK had taught me the meaning of love, unselfishness, adventure and living life to the fullest, being positive and going for it all... for what one believes. She did it all and I learned it all from her. She was my wife and lover, but that was just the surface, the beginning of it. She was more so the mentor, the guiding light, the patient guru who had a purpose on earth, in life above and beyond the selfish and egotistical purposes that humans are driven to follow. Her love, generosity and giving were abundant, without boundaries and open to all. Everyone she had touched or came in contact with her walked away with a smile, a lesson, or a better perspective. She made so many friends and so many places. She had a family here but had a whole tribe and following in the distant land of Morocco. My family loved her, my mother adored her, even the Imam at the mausoleum in the holy city in Fes touched her face and said "you are a blessed child!" She loved and loved deeply, but she had to die at such a young age. Why is that so? How is it possible that a person full of vibrant and positive energy can get so little time on earth to accomplish things? There is no simple or satisfactory answer. We are to assume that the Maker knows best and has surely a design and a plan for all of us once we depart from earth. In my faith, it says that if the Lord wants to lessen the burden and punishment of the hereafter for a faithful, he gives him or her a little "test" here on earth. He or she shall be free of pain and suffering in the hereafter; he or she shall be amongst the dwellers of Lord's paradise prepared especially for these God chosen people.

She lived fully, she has accomplished so much in the last few years alone. The way I saw it, she had lived the lives of three or four altogether in some forty plus years. She was like a candle that burns so vibrantly, yet burns out quickly as it lights the world around it. Why the rush to achieve so much, to go to so many places, to buy houses, to invest to learn yoga? I believe that she knew she was on a short term life span. Something inside of her told her that she needed to do it all and fast because her lease on life would be drawing to an end. Not that she wanted it, nor did she fully understand it, but she had to walk as it was not hers to plan or decide. Unbeknownst to her, it was hers to walk through and see, it was the Lord working through her. She is missed. I am going to miss her so much, I am going to be sad for a long time to come. God help me!

I did not get the chance to say a word during our wedding from 3 years ago; I felt kind of unfulfilled not having reflected enough on my relation with my beloved MK… as the Lord had wished it to occur, I had given a better speech at her funeral, at a moment to me that mattered more. I was simply compelled to reflect back, ponder on the meaning of it and above all draw a lesson from all of it, a lesson that she certainly wanted to teach but time did not permit, and her passing came too soon, but I felt that she was speaking through me, that her words were sounding in the back of my mind. I simply had to utter the words and they flew out of my mouth.

A young man, a guest of my friend Hassan whom I did not know at the time, has reminded me ever since and for years of how much he was touched by what I said, and how much he has learned to cherish family and friends ever since, realizing that those things can be taken without notice as it was the case for me. I saw tears on the faces in the audience and I just bawled, having to sit down as my knees could no longer hold my body up. The moment was too heavy for my body and soul alike.

Some of the misguided people in our circle have the awful idea that cremation of the body is somehow an acceptable way for the body to go to its Maker. And when the body is smoldered and reduced to ashes then it can be sprayed over the ocean. Apparently her father and grandmother passed in that manner, but I just cannot imagine that there is any beauty in such a spectacle, nor do I see the romance in it. Some people actually use the method, and there is no telling if my beloved MK's family subscribes to this because of the lesser financial burden it offers. This is such a warped logic, as if incinerating the body as if it were in the hell fire were a better way.

I am a true believer in the Lord, at heart and in spirit, and even if I did not practice as much, it doesn't matter. The Lord is merciful and wise and when he says that we were created from earth and we shall go back to it, he meant true salvation and blessing in the practice.

Otherwise, there is a hell fire that is reserved for the unbelievers and God's enemies. I leave the comment open and give no description to whom falls under it; I do not know. But the picture of hell and fire are certainly not synonymous with any beauty. I believe that the soul does not leave the body so immediately after death, it dwells in its surroundings and rises or flies away only after days have passed, up to 40 days in the Islamic belief. Incinerating the body during this time is like subjecting the soul to punishment when it is longing for light, salvation, and redemption. What an awful fate that is and how unjust, awful and ungodly a thing to do to a loved one. Love truly does not burn; love cherishes nurtures and grows. This is exactly the spirit of the Islamic burial that I gave my beloved MK.

We headed out to the mosque for the prayers. In accordance with Islamic tradition we stood out outside, lined up shoulder to shoulder for the prayers. Others showed up even though they were not part of the prayer group. Imam Tariq, a great young man of Pakistani origin, was surprised to see the size of the following and certainly did not expect Christians to be present. Without hesitation, he declared that the prayers are also opened and permitted to Non-Muslims, granted that they stand in the back and make rows as the Muslims did. I have not seen Muslims and Christian pray at the same time and in the same place. He simply asked that the Non-Muslims recite from their own belief or simply make a silent prayer while he conducted the ceremony. Awesome indeed.

It was happening before our eyes, without a plan or rehearsal, guided by some magical arm or heavenly will. We were witnessing a ground breaking moment that none of us—the living—had anything to do with. Was Mary orchestrating the whole thing, as she did in life, breaking barriers and defying customs, and making new ones based on love and spirituality?

Another wonderful thing occurred at the Mosque. Other Muslim faithful who happen to be praying at the time took part in the ceremony. People who had nothing to do with MK or me felt compelled to touch her coffin, to catch a bit of the blessing bestowed by the Lord on the departing soul. Beautiful is the word. I am sure MK was soaking in it all as she was being blessed by many loving people.

The grave site was the final resting place for my beloved MK so the ceremony there was one of ultimate joy, bliss and holiness. No exaggeration, no one has, nor any will ever see such a beautiful thing in their lifetime. The ceremony merged two faiths that stand in opposition according to today's events and recent history, which are not based on the true spirit of either religion. Both are God revealed and ordained, but the love and joy that was in it was awesome. Men and women from both faiths made prayers, said words and thoughts and touched the body. Alan, MK's brother, not a Muslim, participated in the whole thing and was simply in awe of what he saw. Although the ceremony was basically Muslim, the faith and its people opened their arms for everyone to take part, share, and invoke their own.

>Nice to have talked over night and over my sleepless soul... I am just worn
>out from all of this, I want something new.. u see i still weights on my
>mind even after I had slept for 10 hours (indeed, I went to be at 4 and
>woke at 12.. it surprised the heck out of me, the boss was nice, nobody
>bothered to wake me up.. good) I just hope I can sleep right tonight..

>Ok lovey dovey, that's it for now.. keep me posted. I love u and my heart is
>closer than ever to you, so do not think that u can hide stuff from OK!? I
>wanna know everything so do share.. let's chat or try to between 9 and 4 pm
>(that's the time I am up.. well I am normally up before 9 but you would be
>still asleep, capice!)

I cannot wait till end of October for our vacation.. work on it please.. but
stay strong first .. ok!)

January 25, 2007

I am still learning how to deal with the hurt of the passing of my beloved MK. I cry on and off throughout the day. Sometimes I feel almost normal, only to realize that the pain, the hurt, the memories and the presence of her in my mind and soul are just too strong. The long road to healing the wounds is just beginning. It is unreal to imagine that my beloved MK is gone. I still don't understand why or how I can live. How can love and energy die at such a young age? I do not understand it. I keep telling myself that my faith will carry me through this. Islam is clear that one should accept the intent of the Lord and harbor no doubts. Questioning the Lord's decisions can lead one astray from the path. No matter how hard the grief and the pain are, one should accept and obey the wishes of God without question. But who has ever loved and cared for someone who wouldn't question this Godly interference? But no, we should pray and meditate to see the good intent of the Lord. But it is not an easy task.

In the holy Quran, Allah says something to the effect that a human being that dares to question the Lord fails to see that the Lord had created him in the first place. These two positions are not on equal footing. There is no room for the created to question the creator. I continue to grieve though my two young brothers are here. They provide me with great comfort. I do not know what I will do when they leave, but life must continue.

Hi Hon...

I miss u so much.. and the more I read Ken Wilbur's book the more I think about u, amazing huh what this experience can do to a relationship. We are forever one, connected together by the souls, but one in the same Spirit, with a big "S"...

OK, now, will u be kind and connect, will u try to stay in touch... pls.. We only chatted once in 5 days and I cannot call u as I wish to and not for a long time to have a meaningful discussion. I only, u can get bugged down with stuff, but make an effort pls.. I need u, I really wanna stay in touch in communication.. u know, I thought about all night.. I cannot stand the separation no more, I am sick of all these soulless places I go to, but more so, my awareness and my growth tells me, I must no longer stay away... so help me come home... this is the feeling that I always langue to, going back home, it is something that puts a smile on my face when think about it.. my heart tells me I need you.. help me ..

love
pooh

Friday, January 26, 2007

Another milestone was reached today; I finally found the strength and time to go to the Attorney's office to revise my Power of Attorney and my Last Will and Testament. I last did this a few years ago when MK was alive, and it was painful to reflect upon the last time we updated our wills back in 2003 and 2005. I remember when we first talked about a Last Will and Testament, we cried over the idea of one of us dying before the other and then of having to live without our best friend and soul mate. We would cry holding each other for minutes at a time; we cried, not knowing what we would do and not knowing what the future would hold. It was exactly what happened, and I was the one chosen to reflect back on the passing of the other. Was it blind chance or a blessing that I was the one who survived? Was it actually a curse? Don't we all like to live and try hard to hold on to life? Am I not the lucky one to live, and enjoy the bounty and the fruit of both our labors? I think guilt is speaking through me, and the devil is again trying to carve up a piece of my peace, faith and sanity. I am not going to let this happen!

I do not understand why MK did not tell me about a lot of things, like the location of the keys to the chess box, a small box that looks like an antique amongst other things that I am finding out in the attorney's office. My little brother Ali says that every one of us has his or her own secrets, prior lives and things that one may wish to keep to one's self and not share with anyone, including spouses and loved ones. I guess I can understand since I have my own little secrets and past relationships, but it still bothers me that I was not privy to some of the little things like the chess box and its contents.

> > *From: Sammy LeBon*

> > *Date: 2005/09/25 Sun AM 03:40:55 EDT*

> > *To: Mary kahthryn*

> > *Subject: Re: Re: To do list*

> >

> > *Hi Babe!!*

> >

> > *I am all ears, heart and soul...*

> >

> > *all I want you to do is HEAL.. how do u do that is another question: I am wondering if u are doing all that needs and can be done for a cure (wholisitic medecine, meditation, accupuncture, balanced diet...etc) stuff that u know already about.. I am wondering if u r surrounding yourself with good, positive and inspirational people!*

> >

> > *When I talked to u yesterday, I did not get that impression I got rather the impression of the Old u, busy with kids, the paulinas.. just busy, bothersome and demanding stuff... u can never be inspired to heal that way (this is at least my impressionand I could be wrong)*

> >

> > *As for other things, I am simply going to surrender; if it happens let it be if it doesn't then it doesn't I am simply not gonna remind you daily of what needs to happen... I gave up, I am human and can run out off patience and u know me to be that way... may be this way (giving u distance and not asking for stuff) u might heal better; i do not know... I am only worried that we fall behind in stuff (paying the bills, insurances...etc)*

> >

> > *Whatever and no matter what I will always love u and with love comes surrender and distance and I give u that too..*

> >

> > *SO, PLEASE HEAL YOURSELF!*

> >

> > *GOD BLESS*

> >

February 12, 2007

Today is the one-month anniversary of the passing of my beloved MK. Another milestone has come and passed. How many more, I ask myself, am I going to go through? I am sure there will be at least a yearly one, and maybe others. Do these things ever end?

I am spending the early morning hours, from 5 a.m. on, going through her emails and reading them, remembering their events and circumstances. I got tired after the first couple of months since there was a lot to go through. We emailed each other a lot since I was on the road for the most part in the last few years. Luckily this past year has involved less travel for me, so I got to spend more time with my beloved MK, and be at her side for the last moments of her short life.

The messages have been largely positive, thank the Lord. I had feared that there would be angrier exchanges among them. MK herself said I had to struggle with anger control issues many times. I am glad the email exchanges were positive for the most part. MK's diagnosis changed my attitude, especially during the last few months as the cancer was getting tougher and tougher to fight and her health deteriorated. MK could no longer rest, and her cancer had taken over by then without either one of us knowing. We believed that there was always going to be a tomorrow, that she had more fight still in her, that in some miraculous way, she would survive and see it through. Allah, obviously, had willed differently from our wishes, but why all the unnecessary pain? I would have been much happier to be at her side, to nurse her and spend her last days on earth with her in peace without the constant agony she was in from the treatment. Wouldn't she have liked that too? I doubt it; the answer resonates clearly in my head, because that's MK. She would go down fighting, no two ways about it, and there was no telling her different... I understand... I do not blame her a bit...

I love you and miss you Babe! It is Valentine's Day, what would have been a nice way to celebrate it this year? We will never know. It is another milestone come and gone.

February 5, 2007

I simply cannot get MK out of my head. Did I say that I miss her so much? I do not know how to deal with it. Everybody keeps telling me that I am doing well, that I am improving, that I am headed in the right *yadayadayada*... do they know how much I hurt? I hurt from the memories, I hurt from the misery she had to go through in the final days, and I hurt for the unsaid, untold words between us. There was so much we could have discussed before her departure.

Don't all people experience the same? Do people really get to tell their loved ones everything? Does anyone settle all issues and have all the conversations that could have been had? Nonsense, I say. It is over before anyone can realize it and the truth is that we are busy with other issues. It certainly was not only that, but who could honestly say that they are waiting for the minute and the moment that the dying are finally dead? I truly thought that a miracle cure could still come from the Lord. Maybe I was in denial, or too optimistic that I wanted to believe that there was a chance, that she would still survive at least a few more days. Love is crazy and hope is crazier.

My brother Ali had a dream of MK. He saw her in her beautiful blue dress, one of the ones that Mom gave her a while back. Just as I saw my beloved MK on the day she passed, he also did, radiant, beautiful and stunning. That is the Mary I know.

In the dream, Ali and I were having a secret conversation and apparently we did not want her to listen in, but she could tell that I was trying to hide it from her. Of course, what else could I expect from my baby MK, she has always busted me whenever I tried to hide something, or not tell her the full story, or flirted with another woman. (This is something I admit doing many times. My Scorpio personality craves female attention… I love my MK, and she knew it, but that is a hard, yet true, statement.)

In the dream, Ali was telling me to be careful, to stop playing around and flirting with other women. As we were talking MK crept up behind him and started, playfully, beating him on the back and shoulders; we were laughing and giggling to signal that we were caught. But when Ali attempted to touch her he couldn't. A small dog kept barking at him when his hands got closer to her. He said to himself "But Mary doesn't have a dog. Wait, Mary is not even alive! I must be then dreaming." It was a sort of half-dream where he was partly awake, or maybe more like a vision in the way we Muslims think of it. Visions can be strange and telling. Forgive me sweetie. I wasn't always faithful to you… but I loved you like no man has loved and like I have never known love. How could I? What an arrogant statement! She told me, no, she taught me how to love because hers was pure, real and heavenly; mine could barely keep up with hers, but still was pure. So pure in fact that I thought I was in love with an angel. Then again, she was one. No doubt, the dear Lord has granted the favors of the purity and particularity of the angels. She was an orphan too.

February 10, 2007

Today, I got up from bed after a night of the usual tossing and turning and insomnia. The memory is simply too vivid and too real to be completely at ease and peace. I remember MK at all times, especially when I am trying to sleep and my brain is wandering amidst memories of her. I am listening to one of her favorite CD's, titled "Jazz Under the Rain." The music is nice, romantic and soothing. They are sounds that we both used to love.

I remember, but what I recall most of the time are very sad images that alternate with very beautiful happy ones. More of them are the sad ones. Do they not say that sad memories are more easily recalled than the happy ones? I believe it.

I keep seeing my beloved MK as she was suffering in agony in the last few weeks as I was constantly trying to comfort her, the signs of pain clearly chiseled into her beautiful face. But she did not want to talk about it herself; she wanted to talk about the medication, fighting the "monster," and the effort to keep fighting. Those last days on earth for her... whose plan was it? Certainly it was not mine neither hers. Allah had willed it that way.

Perhaps the Lord did not want us to share the agony, the pain and the torment of the words we would have spoken had we talked about her certain passing. What can someone say to a loved one in those circumstances? What is it you say or feel in those times? How could one stay positive, knowing the end was near and certain? Perhaps that was the best way of doing it. We fought, lived, talked and interacted as we were still in it, as if tomorrow was always going to be there to improve or at least to fight another day. As if the monster was always at a distance and that his final blow could always be avoided. We fought until we could no longer fight, and the end was short. I thank the Lord for that.

Said Nedlouf

Hi Hon...

I am now at the other place after a grueling but fun couple of days in Amsterdam.. it was so nice to be out and about like normal people... did u get my pics/video from there??

OK, we need to stay in touch and heal- both of us- I was mad, pissed and void for thoe couple of days.. I don't know how to describe it, as much as I love u and feel u and feel the need that I must be near in mind and heart to support and help u through these rough roads.. Despite of it all, I was just crushed n had no desire to deal with you..

I AM SORRY.. I should always rise above it all.. no matter how difficult it gets!

OK.. we will chat and talk over the ph. soon...

love u and miss u
Said

[Mary] wrote:
No No nO I do not want distance from you. You are the most wonderful inspiring greatest person I know and will ever know. You I need and I need help to become better. you can help me. I surrender please help me.

> >
> > Mary kahthryn wrote:
> >
> > >

> > > From: Sammy LeBon

> > > Date: 2005/09/22 Thu PM 01:27:11 EDT

> > HI,

> >

> > Every chemo treatment takes a beating out of my body. It is pure toxic poison. I ssssswore I would never take this stuff when I was healthy. I would rather die. But my will to live is very strong.

> >

> > This last one was an exceptionally hard, I feel like my body is a punching bag. My lower back went numb, I couldn't feel the sensation of touch on my back.. I have that skin crawly, plus going to explode feeling. I am so swollen that I clothes are uncomfortable. I just want to wear my lil Moroccan dress.

The alien in my left breast is causing sharp pain. I am sleeping a lot.!!!

> > all my body wants to do is sleep. I can sleep all day and night.

> >

> > This is the worst one so far. I am crying all over the place. I just do not have any motivation, or energy to do anything. no appetite either I ate a bowl of soup yesterday.

> >

> > I don't want to worry you I am fine other wise.

> >

> > THe only thing that really matters to me is people. Nothing else is impoortant only people.

> >

> > I love you

> >

> > I am going to make some breakfast, maybe I will eat.

> >

> > bye

February 14, 2007

I love you and miss you Babe! It is Valentine's Day, what would have been a nice way to celebrate it this year? We will never know. It is another milestone come and gone.

If you have lived on, what would you have named your child, our child? Where would he have had his – or *her* school? You always wanted a girl. Where would we have had your next birthday? Where would we have vacationed this year? Where would have been our retirement home, city or state or country been like? We will never know that either. I do know, for sure, that we shall both dwell in the paradise of Eden that the Lord, Allah, has promised to the faithful. Beyond the faith, my instinct tells me that I shall meet my beloved MK when I pass on as well, and we will fulfill all her and my dreams too. I guess we will have the answers soon enough, but I cannot help but wonder what you were thinking, what was going through your mind? My beloved MK.

Sometimes during the last month prior to her passing, she would drift into solitude, keeping to herself and sink in some deeper inner soul searching. I knew this, but I did not dare interrupt her moments to herself. Now, in retrospect, I wish I had asked the question "Honey, what are you thinking about? A penny for your thoughts!" Did she really foresee her passing to come, and make her peace with her life on earth? Did she already know that she was on her way out of earthly life? Did she know that the end was imminent, and was making her preparation in peace, quiet and privacy? I know she was simply too kind, too spiritual and too angelic to put me in a situation where I had to worry. How else do I explain her distance? My instinct tells me so, and I hope the fact that I have spent all those years with her means that this is what she was doing. Her dignity, her pride, and her somewhat overly private nature forbade her from sharing those types of feelings. I just can't help but think that, in part, she did not think I was worthy or ought to know about that deep place where she goes alone, in privacy. I blame myself in part for that. I even consider myself at times not worthy of her, all of her. She was a better person than I could ever aspire to. I love her humbly. I will have to simply accept and respect her motives and consider myself lucky that I had the opportunity to spend nearly 20 years in her blessed company.

Said Nedlouf

February 14, 2006

HI baby,

How was your travels last night?? What time did you get home; I trust it was a smooth journey.

I hope it was smoother than mine. The plane was delayed b/c of bad weather. I finally arrived home at 3:15 am. Yeah. It gave me better understanding and compassion for you and all that you go through. You are Super Honey!!!!!

I woke up this morning just hollow and achy, I miss my Honey bunches.

You gave me the best weekend, one that we will remember for the rest of our lives. I t was Awesome!!!!!!!!!

Thank you, thank you, thank you
I love you soooooooo much baby

February 22, 2007

Today marks the 40th day after the passing of my beloved MK, a special day. In accordance with the Islamic faith, the 40th day marks the end of the mourning period. The soul of the dead would have risen to the heavens and to wherever or to whomever it wants to meet. This also marks the end of the time that the soul remains inside the body, which is now decaying faster.

The soul would have gone through a difficult time, going through, and hopefully passing, a rigorous and possibly painful testing as the angels from the heavens ask the deceased all kinds of questions. In our Islamic belief, the hereafter with its promised hell and heaven has started already at this stage of the passing. It is still only a preliminary test; the real test comes on the "Day of Judgment." I am not sure about all of the details as I have never been that religious myself, but I have a general idea. The angels ask questions about the faith and beliefs of the dead, whether he or she believed in the one and only God, and I thank the Lord that my Mary, before her passing, definitely believed and I had made sure that she did.

In her eyes, I saw that twinkle, the understanding that her beliefs had to be tightened and polished in order to meet the Maker with the full confidence and serenity of her choice to go to the heavens and close her earthly chapter. She has always done the right thing, there is no doubt nor were there ever any in my mind. Next to her heart, deeds, thoughts and love, I am dwarfed to nothing. What made me so self-righteous to think that I could make her better, or guide her to doing the right thing with her faith?

I guess something deep inside told me that there was a missing piece there. We talked so much about faith and religion. While she was not religious, she was still a very spiritual being. I was not religious either, but I was a Muslim by faith, while she was howeverChristian Catholic, and practiced her religion less than I practiced mine.

The issue of religion, faith and the hereafter was never settled between us through all the discussions we had. Our discourse was left unfinished, among the many hanging discussions-to-be-continued. We did not need to finish it, anyhow. At the time of her passing, however, the issue had to be resolved, and the question of religious faith, for once, had to be answered: What faith she was to be buried under, Muslim, Christian or other? I had to choose because she could no longer do it. I had to choose because I knew her heart and mine are one and alike; her spirit and mine are together, my soul and hers are in harmony. Does it then really matter how she goes? Yes, and No.

I'll answer the *No* part first. The Lord knows what lies in the heart of men, period. She was still a person of the book, a Christian who believes in God. She was a faithful being. As for the *Yes* part, all men and women should go in the blessed way of God, a Muslim way that is, especially when they were given the choice and made one. Mary was given the choice by her association with me, a Muslim. She could no longer ignore the fact that she was faced with the choice of a faith, Muslim, Christian or none…and the Lord wants us to do the right choice, which is crucial for the ultimate fate in the hereafter. It is mandated for those who are lucky enough to receive the message and enlightenment of God to make a good choice. She got the message and made the right choice by God. I made sure of that; she accepted the faith of Islam. Never mind that she has always had a soft spot for Islam, my religion. She believed in it in her way: she went to the mosque with me, she prayed and even fasted sometimes, and she truly believed more in the last days. I wrote the supplications and I read them to her, and together we prayed and prayed and prayed. We, together, believed in the ultimate, assured and blessed reunion that is to come after our lives on earth have ceased. This can only happen if, together, we go to the hereafter in the blessed way of the Lord, which is the Muslim one.

This is the knowledge that I have of the hereafter. It is based on religion because that is the only way I know. It is the only reference that we humans have. In religion, nobody has come back from the dead to tell us any better or different way. The eastern religions treat death and the hereafter differently, and if they have no proof either then what to believe? We must trust our intuition... which is faith. Hers and mine are the same. Mary however, did not have enough time to let the idea mature, nurture and materialize to make up her own mind. I had to do it for her. As we sat together that day, she was lucid and clear minded despite the atrocious levels of pain. But God, she suffered. Why Lord?

So we talked, and I reminded her that I wanted her to do it for *her*, to accept the religion of Islam, to verbalize the Shahadah, (i.e. the bearing witness to the Lord Allah), "There is no God but God and Mohammad is his slave and messenger...," and to bear witness to all

53

his messengers and to the Day of Judgment. She did, as she repeated those words after me. I could clearly see that she was in complete symbiosis, mind to mind and heart to heart. We felt at that moment that we were blessed by the Lord. Her passing was blessed in the Muslim way. Everyone who attended the funeral was moved and delighted by the beautiful service, not as much for the decorum and rituals, but more so for the presence of good spirits and total absolute love and acceptance and the hand of the Lord guiding to the whole thing. No one had imagined, planned, or conducted the event, it was all driven by the unseen hand of God and, yes, no doubt, the unseen spirit of MK. It went without a hitch, just like her wedding. We honored faiths, beliefs, traditions and beings. It was wonderful. It felt as if Mary was still orchestrating her death just as she did her life. She is an angel, my angel, I can no longer forget her, I have no choice but to live and dwell in her memory. I am blessed…

Hi cara mia (my dear)

Oh cool.. soo coool.. to finally see the family (Ieno & Mario) good.. give'm my love and make sure they stay in touch for the future... may be we can go back you and I one day..

No problem, I could not go to bed when you cried the other night on the phone, so I got up and once again I changed my itinerary... Hon.. I cannot stand the thought that I am away on vacation while you are being tormented in hospitals.. I am going to be by your side and we'll see this one through too..

Love
Pooooh

PS. I 'll be at the airport to pick u up incha Allah, Thr. @ 11pm

PS. love the pic inside the plan, Rose and I think you looked adorable. today, I am watching world cup at Hassan's (Attar) so thank God no fire works, family crap, just simple pleasures of Soccer..

See you soon....

March 4, 2007

This was yet another milestone. How long will I be marking these? I don't know, but I have a feeling it will be a long time before full closure is in sight, if it ever comes.

Today, the granite bearing the title *Mary Nedlouf, 1964 – 2007* was put in place over the grave. A tearful, yet healing and blessed experience. I was honored to witness it. Whenever I am in her presence I feel better. My prayers and my tears: these are the healers my heart needs to carry on. Carrying on is all I can do now.

Carrying on is my objective for the coming days, to avoid breaking down. I am continually amazed me how much I need her, how much of an impact she had on me, and how much she had become part of me, and I of her.

How do I carry on? Sometimes I even cherish longing for her, the sadness of missing her, and the painful memories of her passing. It is weird, yet amazing and I can only explain it in the way that I feel it because it is irrational. It hurts.

The sadness and misery of her passing reaches to the depths of my being. They are the strongest emotions I have ever experienced. I feel that they put me in connection with a more essential me that lies beneath the surface. Mary had always been able to get to that hidden and intimate part of me; she alone knew how to get there. Even in death she is able to find that place. I can connect with the real me, and that can only be good no matter how painful it is.

Barbara is Mary's friend. Mary used to refer to her as her soul sister. Barbara told me during this last visit to the grave site that Mary is an angel that is now watching over me. I say that she has always been an angel sent to earth from the heavens.

This is not a cliché! I know and feel it, and I know how to know it and feel it; I believe I have a gift for feeling, judging by intuition and tapping on spiritual energy that I believe that very few understand, feel or realize. This is how I know that she was a rare being.

She always felt that she was meant for something bigger. She always felt that her experiences were foretelling of an unusual, God-driven destiny. When she was little, she had a traumatic event when she fell from a higher floor in her house, and was consequently told that she might not be able to walk and that she would need to use a walker to get around. She adamantly refused the idea, and told everyone that she would heal herself and *run*, not walk. And a few days later, she actually did get up from the bed and ran. She became quite the accomplished athlete later in life and was on the swimming team in high school. When she was no more than 6 or 7 years old, she would walk to different churches and services as if she knew that there were more to worship than what she was told.

In a moment of clarity, my heart tells me that I need to find a way to live up to and honor the legacy of my beloved MK. I pray to the Lord, Allah, that I will find that way.

March 7, 2007

I was tossing and turning at four this morning, unable to sleep. Ideas and thoughts were running through my mind, when it hit me. This is it, this is what I need to do, this is the answer to my inquiry to what I should do and how to honor my beloved MK's memory. What I needed to do to be worthy of something other of a simple grave with a date on it with the facts of my life.

I'd need to promote understanding, respect and coexistence of the two religions that MK and I come from. We are two living souls, with commonalities, differences, hopes and wishes, plans and dreams. We shared much between us. We shared our religions beautifully. We saw our differences as an opportunity to learn about each other, to advance our knowledge and become better people, which I think we accomplished. Against all odds, I am sure that others can do the same thing. It will take dedication, effort and an open mind, but it can be done. We did it after all! It will be challenging, but what an accomplishment it will be to see others benefit. It shall be done. Watch for what is coming.

March 9, 2007

I did today's Friday prayer at the same mosque where part of my beloved's funeral took place. I spoke to the Imam Tariq and have an understanding and agreement to have a discussion group, a forum between Christians and Muslims. I will share my experience, and the Imam will shed the light on the elements that unify both faiths and encourage both communities to follow suit, with positive teaching, promotion of good faith bases of both religions, and to reject destructive and misguided voices on both sides. So help me God! I am soliciting the help of Mary Barbara, MK's cousin, who had been, and still is, a big part of this endeavor during the life of Mary, her passing and the aftermath. It will be a beautiful thing to have our friends involved in the spirit of reviving, cherishing and honoring Mary. We will take part in the walk for to cure cancer in Tampa, Florida. It will be another milestone for my heartache's cure.

In the end of life there should be a lesson, full of meaning and hope for the many lives the deceased has touched and beyond. It is not an unlucky event, a date on the calendar or a simple memory. I am hoping that I become a better person having gone through all this. I am hoping that the people whom my beloved MK used to call family, friends and relatives are better as well.

March 31, 2007

One day until April Fool's day. What did we do last year for this occasion? I don't remember exactly. I was probably in that ugly, soulless Washington DC awaiting my fate with work. I will not dwell on that memory.

As I sit at Panera's near our house, I cannot help but remember my beloved MK and I coming here for a cup of coffee on a weekend like today. We used to come here every day to people-watch. One day while there, MK met a woman who knew someone who had breast cancer. I think she was wearing her Pink October Breast Cancer Awareness T-shirt. I am wearing the same T-shirt now to get myself psyched for the October Breast Cancer walk. There is a lot of work and preparation left to do to prepare for the event, not the least of which being fundraising for team "Bubbles of Love." MK used to sign her letters, emails and card with the expression "Bubbles of Love." Love was her word, what you always received in her presence, whether you asked or not. Love was her. Before then I will also be participating in the family 5K run which will take place in late May. I ran in it last year and MK was there to cheer me on. She was so wonderful at that; she would do everything she could to make sure that I did my best. How unselfish of a person she was....

The pain lingers on of course. Tomorrow I will go to her grave for my weekly Sunday visit. It is a major outpouring of emotions and thoughts. It is equally pain and healing for me. I read the Quran, I supplicate, and I cry. I ask MK to let me know with her ever-present spirit what I am supposed to learn, think and do. Most times it isn't easy to do, especially regarding future decisions.

I keep telling myself that I have to move on, I have to realize that there is little I can do to affect things, and that I can only guess what MK would do. And how could anyone guess what the living is thinking, much less the dead? It is absurd.

Even so, I think to myself that if I truly listen and try to connect with the spirit of my beloved Mary, the answer will come to me, clear, decisive and timely. But I do not listen sometimes. I've been accused of not listening before. I want to honor her and her spirit, and we will make the run a great thing. The dialogue we are building between Muslims and Christians will also further Mary's legacy. I am considering starting a charity in Morocco in her name, to advance women issues or to draw attention to the plight of orphans. God help me, I want to be able to say that I am an honorable man worthy of having shared her life and her memory. I hope that she will always remain the guiding light for any endeavor that I undertake.

The pain remains, especially when I look at pictures of Mary or think of her. She is ever-present in my mind and soul. My mom told me the other day that perhaps it would be wiser to hide the pictures because of the emotions they trigger. But I find that I am still unable to part with those feelings. I don't know, I hope I am not coming to see joy in pain. I ask the Lord to show me the way.

I have lately been considering leaving it all and going back home to Morocco for a fresh start. It would be a huge move and a life-altering experience. Why should I not? The person that has made America home for me in the last 20 years is gone forever. I have no more attachment to my house, surroundings, relatives and friends. Mary was the center of it all, my reason for being here. Everything revolved around her. My life feels like a void. I have been in complete darkness in her absence. I feel neither joy nor desire in living here.

I do not care for her family without her. I don't even care for my own friends without her. I have known them, either before or after her, but always around her. It means nothing to me to be in a crowd of friends without her. I feel no pleasure in being around her family when she is not there. Most everything I did was with her.

I do not know how to carry on from here. I am lost in a constant haze and fog, unable to steer to light. Perhaps the answer is to finally go home.

It amazes me how these equations have turned out. I spent the first 20 years of my life in my native Morocco, the second 20 in the USA, and perhaps the next 20, the middle age years, back in Morocco.

I don't know. All I know is that I have no longer have the desire to carry on here. I have to distance myself from this place, as did Mary. Perhaps she is telling me to do so. We have discussed it in the past and, as much as she loved the abundance of this country and being with her family and relatives, she has always encouraged me to go back home, even if it might have to be alone. How unselfish! It never crossed my mind. I have always known that we will be together for eternity, both in life and the hereafter. I guess it will have to be in the hereafter. Of course, I still have her in soul and spirit and that, with the help of the Lord, will remain constant and forever.

March 30, 2007

It's midnight. I cannot fall asleep, so I am writing again. Writing about my beloved MK, writing about us.

I am listening to the voice of Fairuz, a leading woman Arabic singer. I've been listening to her since I was a young pupil. Her voice is amazingly sweet and soothing, and her message is beautiful and inspiring, but sad at times. This is what drew me to her music as I am going through my own sadness. In one of her songs, she talks about her lover and how she hid a letter from him. The lyrics go like this:

I write your name, my darling, on the old tree
You write my name, my darling, on the sand in the street

And tomorrow when it rains on the broken stories
Your name will remain, my darling
And mine will be erased

This is what I intend for my beloved MK. Long after I am gone, people will still talk about her. She has touched the lives of many, and no doubt her legacy will live on for many years to come, long after my earthly life vanishes. She is rightly deserving of that honor. She has taught us all lessons of love, compassion and courage beyond the normal. What a wonderful being.

We were together and that was normal as if it was never going to cease. Not worried about tomorrow. Suddenly, we were worried; very worried. We were scared that it will end and it became a real fear all of a sudden. We started to look around; looking for protection or standing guard as if fearing an assault from nowhere; the unseen and the unknowable.

The lurking threat, the enemy indeed came to be and they were very real and very scary. And then the sudden unfortunate realization that this beautiful thing may well be doomed to vanish and stop abruptly!

Fairuz says it well in another song:

I asked you, where are we going baby?
Leave us here and let the years pass us by
if we met and its forever, why are we scared?
every time I see you, is like I'm seeing you for first time
each time we say goodbye, is like it's our last goodbye
tell me, who are we, and why are we(looking around) scared,
and from whom (we are scared)?
tomorrow is our date, and tomorrow is late, do you think it's not coming?
I see you baby, in the clock, in its tickings, coming from nowhere
Oh life, rain jasmine on those who have met and they don't know
From whom they are scared
I asked you, where are we going baby?

Very often I reminisce on the last days of her life on earth, and I still ponder and think about what she was going through as her suffering mounted, and her life dwindled. I knew that she knew in her heart of the inevitable that was lingering around the corner, the ghost of death waiting, and the angels preparing for her glorious passing to the other side. She wouldn't talk to me about it, and it is painful to sit here and guess why.

Was I not worthy of the information? Did she simply want to spare me the pain? Or was she just in a fighting mode? My MK, she is no quitter and would fight to her last gasp. Did she want to keep it all inside? Was she already on her way to the other side and felt that there was nothing else to say, that no one would understand?

Or did she want to limit the spectacle and the drama that others would find in her display?

It must have been such a lonely place to be in, to keep it all inside no matter how painful and hard things were getting. It seemed that as the pain and desperation grew, she grew equally lonely and introspective. She would sit and meditate in a very quiet and somber way. I would hold her and hug her, but she would keep her eyes closed in meditation. We often sat at a bench in one of those quiet and sad parks in the northeast in the cold of winter. It was not romantic at all; they were sad and dreadful. I would read a book, talk on the phone or do exercises, but she sat there quietly for hours at a time. Where did she drift to? What was she seeing or imagining? I will never know.

I am confident that her silence meant no ill intent toward me. She must have done it out of love and compassion. I know this because she came to me in a dream, shortly after her passing, and told me so. This is when she said to me to not worry and that it will all be fine. It was just like her, positive in all circumstances and times, even as all hope was lost for life on earth and death approached. God bless you Baby! How did I ever imagine that I could find a better soul mate than you? That I could live without you and find happiness? I just hope that I can carry on until I meet you again.

Another idea that our friend Barbara offered, over a glass of beer with tears in her eyes, was that I should keep the charm bracelet that MK liked to wear as a memorabilia of our travels. She wanted me to keep it for the future daughter, the one that MK wanted to have. I am much in agreement.

I remember one evening I was in the city of Bucharest, Romania. I was working and did not have a chance for free time, not even to leave the compound where I worked. So when I could go, it was great to be out and mingle with locals at their local hangouts. I was alone, as I was most times when I am traveling, but I had stopped at a bar, a kind of trendy joint in the downtown. By the time I stopped I had had few beers and was feeling a bit tipsy. As I sat to sip my beer, alone, looking at the crowd of people gathering, chatting and drinking, I realized that I was alone. I felt completely alone, and for the first time it hit me, that I am not happy being alone, at all.

I saw then a poster on the wall, an advertisement for a movie. The title was *Filia den Jersy* which translates as "a little girl from Jersey." I believe the main actor was Ben Affleck. The look on the girl on the poster was precious; she couldn't be more than 5 or 6 years of age. She had her hands crossed as she looked up to Ben Affleck; they were both smiling.

I suddenly got teary eyed looking at the poster. I could really feel the connection and love exuding from little girl's smile. There was pure love in it. There is such a magical and angelic thing about children and the connection they have with their parents. There is unconditional love and unspoken feelings. There is a part of the child that is in the mind and body of the parent, and likewise, part of the parent is shared with the child. We did not get to have that.

There is a part of me that longs for the paternal love for a child. I am not fulfilled without it; I simply need it. With tears running down my cheeks, I picked up the poster and inscribed a little message to my beloved, that I wanted my beloved Mary to bear my child, that it would be my greatest accomplishment ever and promised that indeed, the birth of a child shall be the end of my life as a vagabond, because I would have the whole world in front me, in the eyes of the little creature brought forth from our flesh and blood. Our daughter together was not meant to be. It was another unfulfilled chapter in our lives, but I can still have a daughter myself. So, I would like soon to have a baby daughter, in remembrance and fulfillment of MK's wish, and so that I can offer her the bracelet and say that it was a gift from an angel who had been waiting to see her birth. As Sade sings, *"I won't pretend that I won't stop living,"* I must myself go on and live. Live in honor, appreciation and love for the one who has meant so much to me and who makes my life, even now, meaningful and worth living. But I must remember that her legacy, our life and love together, and my future will mean nothing if I fail to become the person that she wished for me to be. To fulfill her dreams and follow on the path she wanted for herself in my company. Oh dear Lord, help me become that person.

April 7, 2007

Oh bird
Oh bird atop of the world
Could you tell my beloved what I'm dealing with?
Oh bird
Go ask them about me to the one who's companion is not with him
He's scarred with the injuries of love
He's there not telling me what pains him
While thoughts of childhood recur in his mind
Oh bird who takes with him the color of the trees
There is no longer anything but waiting and boredom
I wait in the sun's eye on the coldness of stone
The hand of separation guides me
I beg your feathers which equal my days
And the thorny rose and the grains of air
If you're going to them and the paradise of love
Take me if just for a minute and bring me back

It is Easter weekend, a very special occasion for us, MK and I. Of course I, as a Muslim, do not believe in the religious aspect of it, but as far as MK and I are concerned, I might just as well be as Catholic as she was because we did it all. We colored eggs, we played with the kids, we had a big dinner, or more accurately, a feast. I did not go to church, but she did sometimes. It was is a very special time of the year for us, and once again, I am doing it alone.

I am having to learn how to live through these special circumstances, holidays, celebrations, and other life events, and cope with the memories and the what-if's, the if-she-had-been-here's. It is a fact of life that she no longer is of this earth and will never be again.

But what can someone do to cope when half of his life is still tied to another being who is no longer physically there?

The answer is, nothing. I will have to learn how to do something different. Either find new interests, or do the same things with other people, such as close family members and good friends. We did have many of those. So, for starters and to usher a new era of life without MK and carrying on positively, I did something that I felt good about, and felt great after I did.

MK has always been a champion of good causes, foremost of which being giving to the needy, to the homeless, and to battered women. It is this last category that I decided to give to in her honor and blessed memory. It was not a simple endeavor, for it required that I go through MK's stuff and pick up items that she would want to give to charity. That is, I must sort through her items and choose the ones I am ready, however reluctantly, to give up.

I roamed through the house and looked around. Most of what kept staring me at me was the clothing items of which my dear MK had so much, too much I once I thought. Of course, she never thought that she had enough, so I guess it was a matter of perception. My beloved MK was always giving things away to people she cared about. That's the generous soul that she was. I remember her clearly picking things from her wardrobe, especially baggy items and nightwear to give to my sisters. (My sisters were a lot shorter and heavier compared to MK's tall and athletic build.) She was generous to extremes at times, and one needed not to ask her for a personal item before she would offer it simply out of the goodness of her heart.

Anyways, with grief and tears, I picked a few items that were hanging in the closet. These were items such as two-piece outfits, pants and dresses that she would wear on an everyday basis. Some of them were new and never worn before, but I felt were items that other women could enjoy wearing. I felt that these items were simpler, yet more meaningful because there were the everyday items that she wore, lounged around and went out with. I saw her in these items more often than in any others. I felt these were worthier to share with the battered women that she cared for. In a way, I am giving a piece of her to these ladies; I was allowing her to be in their company, in spirit, since the clothes, despite missing the body that wore them, embodied her spirit.

As I was holding the items on a cart, I touched them and said goodbye. I smelt some of them; her blessed sent was still there. I was in tears but knew in my heart that it was the right thing to do, and it was time. The grief counselor mentioned that the decision of letting go of some of MK's items is solely mine. There is no set time or appropriate way to do it, it was all up to me and the way I felt about it.

I thought it would be an easy thing to do. I was convinced that I should give her items to charity and some, of a more personal nature, to close friends and family. But as the moment neared for me to part with them, it became really difficult, and found the experience emotionally draining. This is not to say that I had any doubts or change of mind. It is part of the healing process that I must go through to get over the loss of my beloved MK. I am still, nonetheless, moved by these experiences where I feel the connection to her spirit so strongly. She is present, no doubt.

The day before, a Friday, I went to her grave site for my weekly ritual. Prior to going, I went to the mosque for the weekly group prayers, which I do not get to do often as I am often on the road. The Imam's weekly sermon was about the loss of life at a younger age, and how does one prepare for life in the hereafter when we are struck with death while young, and believe that we still have a whole life ahead. It was a very tough subject, and the sermon hit me very hard.

The Imam mentioned something that is similar in all other revealed faiths, including Judaism or Christianity, the idea that life on earth is passing while life in the hereafter is eternal. One must keep that fact in mind as one lives his earthly life. One must not plan so much for this life since it is truly short lived. A seventy, eighty, or even one hundred years life span is still short compared with life in eternity. One does not take along his or her belongings when they go meet the Maker, yet, most will strive for possessions in this flimsy, fickle and meaningless life. The Imam quoted from the holy Qur'an to what approximates to this meaning[2]: *Allah says: "...and when it reaches the throat and he thought that it was the separation, and the leg tied to the other, on that day to your Lord you are dragged..."*

---

[2] This approximation is the best definition that I can give. I note here that it would be a sin for me to translate the meaning of the Qur'an improperly.

The Imam explained that when the soul reaches the throat, as it is the last organ or point from which it is leaving the body, one might still think they can still live on. Thus the words "he thought that it was the separation." To explain, some people with less faith would still fight the ultimate fate dictated by the Lord that they are called upon to leave the earth. They have illusions that they can withstand their fate and live on, which is wrong. It is also a torment for the passing not to give in, surrender and accept their fate as the Lord has already predestined to them.

My beloved MK surely wanted to live and fought as hard as she could in those final days, but I have the confidence that as a true believer, she had the presence of mind and heart to accept her fate in those dire and hard times prior to her passing. I also had faith that those moments turned peaceful and blissful as she knew she was about to undertake the awesome, blessed, beautiful journey ahead. I pray and believe that she did indeed accept her fate and give up the battle that was no longer hers to fight, and that the Lord relived her from the pain of it all to replace it with the serenity and calm of the journey to the hereafter.

The Imam also mentioned that the fate of the human being, not knowing when the Lord might call upon to join him, is such that he or she must be in a continual state of preparedness to pass to the afterlife. How does one accomplish such a thing? Isn't it against human nature to abandon life and earthly matters? Aren't we supposed to enjoy the bounty that the Lord has provided for us to enjoy? I would think that the answers we come up with are personal answers, and that the decision of how to live our lives is a personal choice. Not so, says the Imam. One must not focus on earthly matters, if one is to honor the Lord. Matters of this life shall always be in moderation. There is no joy or glory in earthly success while others, close and distant, are suffering. One must keep one's desires and ego in check at all times, because they do not know limits. But the limits are still there nonetheless, and we can choose to observe and honor them or we can choose to live "like animals," and obscenely over-indulge in matters of life.

Just as the Lord knows our ultimate fate, he also gave us the choice in making decisions that would lead us to that ultimate fate. One might say it is a paradox or contradiction, but if we break it down to simpler thoughts it becomes clearer. Live life in moderation; do for yourself, for others and for the Lord. The ultimate fate is known and has never changed; we will all die one day.

There is a reckoning ahead, a judgment day if you are a believer. Otherwise this life on earth serves no purpose, and how could that be possible? There is a Maker, someone outside of us, outside of the universe, outside of matter, because he is the Maker of the matter. Even science as advanced as it is in our times has found limits to its logical reasoning, and cannot explain how the universe was created. Neither can it recreate the smallest of God's creations after discovering its genome. Anything that is made is created by someone or something outside of it; the universe, in its infinity, cannot have been made by itself; it was created by the Maker who was outside of it and who is not bound by time, matter or concept. So in the end, life is precious, has meaning and is worth living the right way.

My visit to the grave site was another blessed event. I got to share my ideas, worries and stories with my beloved MK. I mentioned to her all the ideas and plans I had for the future. But I was also struggling with my anger towards her family and especially her mother. I had so many questions and did not expect to get all the answers at once. But I did get a few: the fact that I gave away the clothing items this morning was a clear sign that MK listened, and guided me to the right decision. After all, this was a personal matter. I always feel great after visiting MK. My grief is lessened and I feel a total calm and rest afterward. She always knew how to calm down with her positivity and kindness. That what I miss most as I now go alone through my days. I guess even in her absence her guidance is still following me, pushing me to the right path, and reminding me of the important things. Just as the Imam said, we must always do the right thing as we are accountable for our deeds.

MK., the Angel at her Baptismal

Our wedding night. I never saw her happier!

MK. always remained cheerful and positive, even as the disease kept winning the battle for her life.

Even in times of pain, the grueling chemotherapy, the loss of hair, and so on, we kept a good sense of humor.

Malak Mariam Nedlouf
Born: 9.1.09
Meknes, Morocco

Kenza Cheryl Nedlouf
Born: 4.17.10
Meknes, Morocco

Forever a Family on 7.27.11
"In our hearts, they were already ours; we simply had to bring them home."

From the pain of loss rises the joy of new love, a new family, and a new beginning.

MK's last birthday celebration on earth, November 4, 2006

Last vacation in Thailand, November 2005

Malak poses behind the heart symbolizing her Angel Mary Flower, as she refers to it.

An Angel in Our Midst

Adoption

Birth defect

Mother (adoptive) (born with all her medical organs on the opposite side of her body)

Mother in & out of hospital for care.

4 5/6 adoptive mother died

Brought to FL to stay with cold people, strangers during my mothers funeral.

6 years old   father remarried a woman ē 2 boys age 3 and 1 1/2.

We moved from N.Y. to Fla.   left everyone that loved me.

7/8 years old   My father & mom took in 2 18 yr old male cousins. They lived with us for 2 years.   During those 2 years The cousins with 2 new brothers would gang up & beat me up, see what they could do to me t make me cry & drown me in the pool.

9 1/6 Playschool friend of brothers died.
15 1/6 Dog died

A Chronology of Pain

9 1/2	a family of 5 00000 children now
	2 new baby brothers.
1/2/6	adoptive mothers father died (Grandfather)
	I have now been the only cherished + adored
	child to the middle then the oldest.
17 1/2	fathers mother died NaNa
20 1/2	father died
	second family dog died
	uncle died uncle bob
22 1/2	adoptive mother's mother died (Grandmother)
24 1/2	uncle Tommy died
25	cousin tommy died
	Eloped
25	started college
25-28	went to work at a restaurant
	one of the owners, sexually fondled,
	hit & verbally abused me & many other women.
29.	took to court., won
	separated in Marriage
	friends lil girl died at 5 1/2

A Chronology of Pain, continued

In college
A close friend & her husband
were brutally murdered

Entered Nursing School.
All Nursing schools are loud, dysfunctional
ego maniac instructors
Discovered I had a learning disability
Pains disorder #a DSM III

2000	Graduated from RN school.
2002	Moved to Orlando from Tallahassee
2003	Became Re engaged to my husband
Aug 31st	Remarried Happy Days!
2004	Started ~~married a~~ Building Some independently.
Jan	
2005	Precious Good Mother died
2005 March	Aug died
2005	~~~~ Robert Best friends Husband died
2006	Aunt Marie died
2005	DX J Ca, IBC
2006	Bilateral Breast Ca.

A Chronology of Pain with some bright moments!

Now I am going to read a lil & go night, night, MaryKathryn.
I Love You so very much ♡

Thank you Dearest Lord for loving me.
Thank you for healing me of cancer.
Thank you God I Am Healed!
You have blessed w/ perfect Divine
Health. All is Good.

Good Morning Lord !!
I slept great last night first time
in a long time. from all the prayers.
My sleep cycle has been scattered.
Going to bed at 0500 then having life wake
you up at 10-11 ohh does not give you/me enough
sleep. I went to bed around midnight
& woke up at 8:30. I have to turn off my
alarm clock set for 7:00. It interrupts my
sleep.
I surrender dear Lord. Thank you for
taking this away from me. I am perfect
Health.

A Good Sleep

Hello Mary Kathryn,

I have this hollow ache in me
but where is it coming from?
It feels like it's over my left side
positioned like the heart at an angle.
It is not physical. My soul aches!
When I am busy I block it out but when
I am doing something mundane like
driving, shopping, watching TV, cleaning
I feel it. Like a beacon light
for ships bringing them home to safety,
I remember in Nursing school the
ache sensation, reminded me of an
axe that came down on my chest.
The pain was so raw deep.
I had this feeling a few months ago
during second Chemo. Then I started
attending the Wed. nighter group.
The feeling would go away for
a few days and then I'd feel it again
by the weekends. Attending Healing prayer
& Wed. nighter helped me sooth the feeling,
plus the daily reading.

Her Pain

I Demand & Is Command, this (BCA mmorganism)
Leave my body Now! Go Back From where
ever you have come from,

May Allah and All the good prayers that we recieve be on our
side and that the dream is Realized.
"the Gates and Skies are open"

Even as she fought the monster of cancer, she still held onto her desire to live and enjoy life.

Love is meant to inspire us with its power

I am inspired to do anything my ♡
desires to make me happy. I am inspired
to fly soaring above any small hurdles
to reach my dreams.

To love all unconditionally

To find the path of love to God

Love is Meant to Give Us Power

Love is meant to make us certain
with out doubt.

I am loved enamously
I am one important player of the
universal energy.
I am, pure consciousness
I am the sender, median, reciever
I am gorgeous
all am I God

Love is Meant to Make Us Certain

Love is meant to make us safe

to go to the pure source of consciousness. the
I am. To relax to trust your esp to be
in love the comforting source of energy, universal
Energy. To be in the light of God. To have
gratituted, Divinely, to know.

Love is Meant to Make Us Safe

Love is meant to oust all fear

That I am alone, issolated, unloved,
Love is meant to oust all fear of
failing, I can never fail anything
I try, attempt to do. Im always
learning. Love is meant to oust all
fear of struggleing, Let Go & let
God! Lift you from your holes you
dug yourself into, let yourself be loved

Love is meant to oust all fear,
all limitations, judgements, boundaries
off and away from ⬤ my spirit,
my self.

Love is meant to oust all fears
So I may live the path of Love

Love is Meant to Oust All Fears

Love is meant to renew

the lost faith and love I have in myself.
Love is meant to renew, rejuvenate, energies
motivate my inner o physical desire for
personal achievement. Saraswati the goddess
of knowledge inspired. Love is meant
to renew my path to love. I am pure consciousness
to truely understand everyone all is spirit
Love is meant to renew my heart to freedom
so I do not judge, label or critize any thing
I accept it unconditionally. Love is meant to
renew pure love.

Love is meant to renew the relationships
I have with other spirits on this earth plane
there are no coincidences so everyone is here
for a purpose.
Love is meant to renew my trust in men.
Love is meant to renew my silence internally
and audio.

Love is Meant to Renew

Happiness is...

Courageously doing what you want to do,
even if you are scared.

Experiencing your life as an exciting journey.

Stimulating your mind and caring for your body.

Realizing that you already have everything you
need to make yourself happy.

Knowing that you are the only one who can
decide what is right or wrong for you.

Accepting that you are okay even when you
blunder and learning from your mistakes.

Knowing that what people say or do is
a reflection of them not of you.

Listening to your inner wisdom.

Giving and receiving unconditionally.

On Happiness

In the jungle of Body, there is a flower i.e. soul, that never dies, that never dries ever luminous, ever fragrant, ever new, everfresh

An ounce of practice is far better than tons of ~~theory~~ theory

Don't think that it's too late this is the time to earn GOD.

Your Breath is my Presence (GOD, Baba

ॐ Namaste welcome

On Meditation

When I did Kriya regularly I did not feel this ache like God washed away. No I was filled c the lords love. Meditation fills me c the lords love. Then I hunger for more love for complete fulfillment.

What is wrong with me, I don't think I love me. Right now I want a cup of Hot tea, lock up the house put an Ice pack in the freezer. But I just don't have any energy. lack lusty. Telling myself it is okay to be tired is not an excuse b/c this does not take any energy.

My house is clean it just isn't straightened 30 min clean up. I do feel so much better if I do this. So please Mary do it. You need to Go to Bed By 10:00 Asleep by 11:00 a normal Routine.

Well I feel Better, I straightened the House, prepared the coffee for AM & cherry on top Exfoliated my face & neck YES!!!

On Meditation 1

flower in head, fontanel, visalize the person to heal.
bring flower with you if leaving for more than 2wks.

<u>Chakras</u>   field of consciousness
Fontanel   hidden presence of God, God center
Medulla   perception of the soul   Soul center
Cervical   Vacuum   Religionosity , Communication,   } 3 highest emotional powers
Dorsal   air   ♡ most Dangerous, Welcome Emotions
3rd Lumbar   Fire   Negative food to E } Animal Centers
7   Sacral   water   Family, sex
1   Coccygeal   earth   Survival

Kingdom of God is 10 fingers width
maintain, truth, inner truth, inner Purity.

5 flavors   5 senses   Astral
fruit   fruit actions, Karma
money   a Physical Body

if you die before you die   , then you didnt die

fontanel goes directly to the p. tuitary
through the Cerebrum, MidBrain, Hypothalmus

On Meditation 2

God rewards the people who seek after him.

Power of ~~Remember~~ Remembering creates faith and hope if used for the right purpose.

Remember all the great things that God has done for you/me.

Psalm 77:11
I recall the many miracles God did far me [how done]
They are ~~constantly~~ in my thoughts.
I cannot stop thinking about them.

Our Victories, Our successes, Celebrate what God has done in my life Happy healthy whole. If God did it once he will do it for me again.
God Blessed me with perfect Health Staying in an attitude of faith just remember you are a Victor not a Victim I have been Supernaturally healed Me God is all Powerful.
God is the Giver of all Good things

April 14, 2007

yesterday we ended so there is no more us or it (Yesterday)
hey promise's owner(her lover) make the promise becomes forgetting
sleep went around your past
and went o life gardens crying so calm down now
farewell was smiles wetted with tears sometimes
and with memories other times
even gifts which was our fortune
we forgot it in the farewell night
hair tape
scent of perfume
handkerchief (napkin)
and a star fell from a branch (of tree) where we used to meet
I gave it to be carried by the earth winds
during gusts so you (talking to the star)didn't get to shores
oh journey in the extent of forgetting that hurts (me)
oh journey in the extent of forgetting that hurts (me)
love didn't need it neither did we
love didn't need it neither did we
yesterday we ended

Another week has passed since I wrote anything. It has been busy here. It doesn't get any easier having to do everything on my own: laundry, bills, repairs, work, and so on. More and more I finding how much my beloved MK was a pillar of support for me. In all honesty, she did most of the things that needed to be done around the house. She was great at the finances and bills. She knew what the various components and parts were of devices around the house, the brands, the deals, how they functioned, and sometimes could even take them apart. When things broke, she either knew how to fix them or who to hire to do it. Let's face it, she built the house herself and knew all its nooks and crannies. All I had to do was bring in a paycheck. I was blessed to have been able to provide for her and allow her to use her own imagination, talents and know-how to work around the house. I am at such a loss without her, and I struggle to get by doing such things. I miss her so much.

This weekend would have been the one we would go and camp with her brother and cousins. I did not feel like doing it for a couple of reasons. Without MK, there was no more fun in doing those things with her family. Many of these family gatherings took on a special meaning for me because of the interaction that MK had with the rest of them, and I was glad just to be a good companion. I truly did not care for the people as I am not much like them, and it was difficult to relate to them. This is not a criticism but rather just a fact.

But I had another objection to these family outings. This concerns primarily a particular member of her family, whom I do not think has the ability to act in a motherly fashion, or display the true loving, caring and sensitive character expected of a mother. MK had issues with that aspect of her life all throughout, and could never understand why that person was so stingy in showing appreciation for the sole female in the family She never understood why she had not been there for her in times where she truly needed a motherly presence and support. She would often invoke reasons such as lack of time, money and other excuses not to acquiesce to MK's needs. But on the other hand she would show more support and compassion for other members of the family, and would spend much more time with them.

One cause—and this is purely my assessment and feeling—may have been the fact that MK was an adopted daughter as far as she was concerned, but that is best left alone. There is nothing to gain or learn from it. That secret died with MK, and I shall let it go as well.

The fact of the matter remains that my beloved MK, who had the biggest and most generous heart in the world, landed in a family where she was misunderstood—that's my opinion again. She was emotionally deprived and starved for love. But MK loved unconditionally. She loved all of her family members just as intensely as she would love anyone else, including me. She did not care for the lack of reciprocity. She did not calculate the amount of love anyone deserves. She didn't make remarks or comments on others shortcomings when they were quick to point out her flaws. She didn't judge or blame, she simply loved, and loved immensely. Love that outshone all the negativity around her. She wins of course!

She was always the first one to call, the first one to send a card, the first one to invite the family for parties, the first one buy gifts, and the first one to give monetary aid. She was the first one to have anything to do regarding to the well-being of her family. Yet when she was on the receiving end she was last, and that remained till the day she died. That is my feeling. I felt it in her words and in her eyes.

Many in her large family were cliquish types. They would hang out in smaller groups that exclude some other family members, and she was excluded many times. They would have their own get-togethers and did not want to associate with anyone else. I am speaking about some particular members in her family. I admit that I don't think well of them. When I vocalized my dissatisfaction with them, MK would forbid it and would simply ask that I give them love and prayers. How generous this angelic person was. I am dwarfed by her emotional and spiritual maturity. I acquiesce, I forgive, I redact, I retract, I give love and ask for nothing. I seek not to understand anymore, rather forgive and go on...

MK was born to different parents from the ones who raised her. She confided that only to a few. In fact, she was so secretive that even her lifelong friend, soul sister and confident, Barbara, didn't know. When I told the story later on, she asked me "Why would Mary keep such a secret?" I answered that perhaps Mary did not to feel any different than any other "normal" sons or daughters who were raised by their biological parents. She did not want to be treated any differently. But as much as she strove to have close relationships with her adoptive family, the doors were often slammed in her face. One cannot change people's natural inclinations; good or bad, they will manifest themselves as coded in their birth essence.

My MK would tell me the story here and there when things got really difficult with the family, in bits and pieces. Here it is plainly: she was born to an Austrian couple who came to study at the University of Florida in the late sixties. Her birth certificate still bears the place of birth in a hospital in central Florida. Her father, having had family already down in the Central Florida area, had learned through a doctor at the hospital that there was a child ready for adoption. The Austrian couple, being students, did not wish for the burden of a child born out of wedlock.

A side note: Isn't it true that all of the prophets and messengers of God were orphaned, mistreated by their own and yet the Lord bestowed on them the most and the biggest gift to give a message of love to the rest of the humanity. MK was such a chosen person in my mind.

MK's adopted father was already married to his first wife from New York. If my memory serves well, this woman was later diagnosed with *dextrocardia*, a birth defect that put her heart on the opposite side of her body, and according to Mary she was often sick. She eventually died, and Mary was to be raised by an aunt in New York. Mary always remembered and spoke at length of the love she received then. While we were in Connecticut for the dreadful treatment, we had a chance to visit some of the family in Staten Island; they were very kind to me, and loving and compassionate towards her. We spent MK's last Thanksgiving with them.

She remembered her trips to old churches and shopping centers during the snowy winter seasons. She was happy in New York. When MK's father re-married and decided to move south to Central Florida it was, as Mary would recount, as if her heart was ripped from her. Her happy days, and the people who truly loved her, were left behind. Mary landed in a cold and distant world, and after that she was never the same.

But MK had love in her heart, even while she was not getting it back. She felt there was favoritism toward the boys in the family. They were four from the new marriage. Her new mother, in a sort of Freudian drama, wanted to compete and win over the love of her father. I am paraphrasing Mary's words here, but this is certainly the feeling that I was getting when talking about the matter with her.

Mary was a spiritual being even at an early age. As she told it, she felt that she belonged to all the faiths. When she was six, she said she often ventured out into other neighborhood churches without a chaperone, sitting down and praying or listening to sermons. She knew by instinct that spirituality and religion were not bound by titles or labels, denominations or sects. Well, she married me as a Muslim, and became a Muslim, in addition to being a Catholic and an adept of Eastern spiritual doctrines. She was all in one, just like the universe. She knew all of this early by pure instinct, I confirm; she was an angel before her time and without knowing it, and her death was nothing but a vehicle to a new journey in the spiritual realm. God bless my angel.

With her death, also has died my desire to associate with her family. I remain true to her spirit in giving them love and prayers as she asked, and I will be polite, but I will remain distant. I have always made generous gestures towards her family in following with MK's desire. In fact MK, without telling me, put her mother on as a co-beneficiary in a life insurance policy that I paid for. I have no issue with this decision. It puts my conscience at ease because it put my Mary's mind and heart at peace as well kept her mother healthy. She stayed true to her caring and giving nature by naming in her Life Insurance Policy someone in utter unselfishness and without reciprocity. They did not even know about it! I pray that the Lord has mercy on their soul; forgive them not for their own sake, but for that of the wonderful spirit of their adopted daughter. I remain humble to consider that the Lord had a good reason for bringing her into her adoptive family. I repent from if I had uttered words of blame. I know it would have displeased my MK if she had heard me. Maybe she has... sorry babe!

True to my ritual, I will now head to the grave site and talk and pray with MK. I must get some peace, because discussion about MK's mother always turns my spirit sour, and I need prayer to recover.

I don't really understand these feelings I have. I cannot even bring myself to converse with loved ones even in my own family. Why is this? I feel a need for solitude. Maybe I feel like I do not have real support from my family and close friends, and therefore I do not need them. If they cannot be there for me then I do not need their friendship. I cannot bring myself to talk to my own brother, mother or other family in Morocco. I feel resentful, like they do not support me. Of course, I appreciate their sympathy and love towards me, I just can't accept the fact they are not able to help. I am not sure that this explanation is valid. I would like also to think that part of it has to do with the fact that I am not able to replace my love and friendship with MK with anyone else, family included. My brother for example, was here for more than a month while MK was in her final days on earth. His time here was taken up primarily with his life-threatening accident. (That's a topic for a later discussion.) As my brother Youssef was getting healed and recovering from his injuries during that month, he showed little concern and less compassion and understanding for what I was going through.

I often say to him that he is emotionally and spiritually immature even though he is knowledgeable about religious matters. Still, he did not call much after he left to go back to his hometown in Atlanta. Neither did he honor my request to stay a bit longer with me in my house to provide me company. He did not really have a life in the Atlanta area, nor a career, nor an education or a good job. In fact, he was in the process of moving from an apartment he shared with three other guys at the same time that I was offering to have him stay for free in my house.

I do not understand him so I simply told myself that he is no longer worthy of my brotherhood or friendship. I believe that my situation is typical of someone who has lost a true friend and is not able to replace her in any way, at least not for now, and not completely. I forgive him and hold no ill intent towards him. I love you Youssef!

My hospice therapist seems to think the same way. She said that I am simply looking inward while being judgmental and reflective about all other relationships. I am measuring my lost relationship with MK by the standards of my relationships with others, which is not reasonable. I need more time to heal, and thanks to the Lord I feel that I am getting better in many respects. It takes time, and my therapist says I am doing well. I believe that my sense of faith and spiritually, which I have learned from MK herself, is guiding me through it all. She is guiding me in spirit herself as well. And of course, the big heart of my mother has never failed me, least of all now. So I am blessed, loved and well taken care of. Praise the Lord.

April 20, 2007

It is one of those of nights of "wide-eyed awake in the dream stage," a bit past midnight. I am, as always, reminiscing and thinking. What's new? I am always with my beloved MK at these times, especially when I come back home on Fridays.

Tomorrow, Carol and Barbara, two of MK's best friends, will spend time with me to sort through MK's things: clothing items, make up and personal effects. This is continuing what I had started earlier, three months after MK's passing. It is still a very painful process, but I am thinking of the good that it does, sharing with those who do not have things.

In fact, today our tenant had stopped by to talk and check in. She was very thankful that I have given her some of MK's clothing items and make up last week. She mentioned to me that she feels like she is walking in MK's shoes, through all the pretty ornate streets that MK had walked in when she was in Italy. Indeed, my beloved Mary had bought the shoes in Italy, because they were very comfortable and because she could not wear anything else. This was also during the time when she was still taking chemo pills. It was a bittersweet period. MK indeed was still in pain, and she also had a deep feeling, that only a person like her would know how to interpret and rationalize. She felt as though she did not have much time on earth to accomplish all of her dreams. She had always wanted to go to Italy with her closest friends.

Indeed, this was a trip that her late father had promised her for her high school graduation. Destiny had it that her dad passed before her graduation.

Things went really sour after that. Her mother could not hold the family together, did not know how to handle the loss of her husband, and did not have enough time in her for MK. This is a very painful memory even for me. I cannot even imagine how MK felt about it. I try to put myself in her shoes and think what it would feel like being without a father and quickly losing a mother. In fact, the whole family moved out. They literally and physically left town and she remained alone behind! So sad to think of that fate.

What made things worse was the fact that her father had passed away suddenly, after a short bout with a disease that he did not reveal to his wife and children. MK felt alone in those times, when she was barely seventeen. Even her grandma, another of those less compassionate people that the Lord had challenged MK with, would not take her in while she got her life together. The choices for MK then were grim. Her mother had asked her to move to Pennsylvania to fulfill a dream of MK's late dad: to live on a farm, raise their own cattle and eat their own produce. This was a great dream when her dad was alive, MK thought, but after his passing she did not feel comfortable moving to a new area, with no friends, places to go, or activities appropriate for a seventeen year old. Of course, her mother would not have any of it, so move she did. It was disastrous. In less than five years the farm was lost. The family dispersed as everyone blamed each other for the failure. Anyway, God bless them, and forgive them all for they did, not knowing how much it did to hurt MK. Who better to quote here than the great one of all, Jesus Christ: "Father, forgive them; for they do not know what they are doing."

The bottom line for now is that I will be giving away more of MK's things, helping to narrow the gap of the immediate memory of her passing. The long-lasting memory of MK will remain forever. I am told that at some point I will miss the painful part of the memory, but I cannot wait for that day to arrive. The pain has yet to subside. I pray that my spirituality and faith will carry me through.

I've been listening to Fairouz's music again. It is beautiful poetry. It makes me feel so emotional, makes me dig deeper into my soul and heart to find the words to describe my feelings towards my beloved.

Do you see how big the ocean is...?
I love you the size of the ocean; I love you
Do you see how far the heavens are...?
I love you, the distance from the heavens (to earth), I
love you my beloved...
I love you my dear
I waited for you... I called you... I painted you
Oh my life's worry, oh the smell of the
rose ...oh the seasons of the birds...

Here is another poem from my all-time favorite Moroccan Band, Lemshaheb, or, "The Flames." This type of music goes back to the late seventies and eighties, at a time where Moroccan pop culture had a sort of awakening. It was for Morocco a kind of counter culture, a rupture with both the then-popular art forms and music from Egypt, and the more-westernized and well-educated French culture that had always been part of the Moroccan art scene. Bands like Lemshaheb successfully brought back Morocco's old pop music that had been forgotten, or simply left to the very old-fashioned and old-minded. These counter culture bands repackaged the art form, the words and the message to appeal to the new generations, the twenty- and thirty-year-olds.

I fell in love with the music and since then it has been part of my musical collection. It appeals both to my rebellious spirit and to my connection to my Moroccan heritage and psyche. But I continued to keep up with more recent trends in art and music. Consequently, this music is kind of left for special occasions when I miss Moroccan music and feel the need to connect back, to reminisce on the past.

Recently however, I have felt a growing need to look back at my old music and get away from the recent memories that current music usually evokes for me. So, as I am looking through the different titles that I have in my music library, I found, oddly, a song that speaks of the trials of dead. A strange idea, but one that hits home with me in my grief. The words painfully echo MK's passing. After all these years I had never paid any attention to the title, but there it was…

This was written and the deadline has come
This was written and the judge has passed his judgment
Allah is great and will judge with what is right
The best of the youth has died in martyrdom
Died at a young age whilst still pleased with life
Died with worries and was full of life
Died but was hoping the way will get straightened
But Allah had already written the destiny
Allah had passed the death sentence
The sentence was done and darkness fell

April 22, 2007

Today was a very interesting and wonderful day. Carol and Barbara came to the house again to look through my beloved MK's stuff in order to sort through more of her belongings, mostly clothing this time. It was another teary-eyed experience for all of us. With each item we pulled from the stacks of clothes that MK have amassed through the years memories came rushing in a torrent, bringing me to tears. Each outfit the girls pulled out had a story attached to it, a place and time when Mary had worn it. Sometimes, Carol, Barbara and I had to tell stories about when MK wore a particular outfit.

I flew down memory lane with much pain and sorrow. MK had always dreamed that she would get better in order to wear those outfits again. She dreamed that she would lose weight to fit into those skimpy outfits that she once wore in the eighties. But that was MK, with so much willpower and drive to accomplish what many would think impossible. She never wanted to throw stuff away. She knew in her heart that there would a time and place again for everything she possessed. Carol tried on a T-shirt and a pair of workout pants; Barbara put on a sweat jacket that MK used to wear in her later days. In wearing some of the items the girls felt that they were walking in her body, in her shoes.

She used to be graceful in many outfits. As the years rolled on and the disease grew harsh she could no longer fit into many of them, but MK could always find a way make herself look great.

We made a visit to the grave site and put on some more ornaments, sprayed water, and read some prayers. While we were there was another burial, for a Muslim man. God bless his soul. I am so lucky to have been there and to have touched his body and made a prayer for him. In my Muslim beliefs, the more prayers you do for the passing, the more rewarded one will be later. We also believe that the passing have no fortune nor baggage that will follow them except for the prayers that people say for them.

It is a very difficult, tense and confusing time when a person passes from the world of the living to that of the dead. There is so much commotion surrounding one at that time, yet the person is very lonely. He or she needs companionship, people to talk to him or her, people who would say a good prayer and supplication for his or her soul. This is why it is a tremendous blessing to be bestowed on one if they are compassionate and empathize with the dead at the crucial time of passing.

I hope that I will be blessed to have people around to say goodbye at the end of my days. My beloved MK had great fortune in having so many good people around her to pay their dues and pray. She is fortunate to have people still think of her in their prayers and sermons. These are the kind of things that she needs now, and the kind of company she can enjoy. I am sure that her spirit sores high to meet whomever she wishes, past loved ones whom she loved and who loved her, and the family and friends that she longed to see and meet again. She is also capable of meeting me. Oh how much I pray that she does, because it is an awesome thing. In the three or four occasions that she blessed me with vivid presence, it was a wonderful experience. We have for sure a great connection that will last for eternity.

April 28, 2007

Oh how large is the forest... so is my heart...
I have a picture of you on my door... your picture is in
my heart
I waited for you for a year... oh how long the year is...
Ask the almond tree...
I see you in my awakening, coming at dawn
But I lose you in the leaves of the Almond tree
Oh how beautiful the smell of a rose
I want to look at a candle and love you

Back from another trip, and back to my ritual. I am once again sad, even bitter sometimes. My emotions are dark at times and the negative seems to win. This reminds me of a verse from a poem written by Al-Mutanabbi, one of Arabia's most famed and celebrated early poets. He was known for his savvy and profound poetry, albeit sad and negative. He wrote the following about his suffering:

My tormentor is always on time, even if death has to
stand in her way
If I had to die with thirst, I wish there
would be no rain after me...

I am not inspired to write tonight but I have to since that tormentor is visiting me also, the pain and memory that engulfs me when I am trying to sleep. I review in my head over and over again the time leading up to the passing of my beloved.

Often, I ask the unanswerable question: why? Why did she have to die? Why couldn't the Lord spare the life of such a wonderful, adoring and God-fearing soul? Another question I ask is: if? If only I had the opportunity to talk to her a bit more, a little longer in those days. I wanted to tell her to be at peace and calm and total serenity as the Lord had a road that has already been paved for her. That she would walk it and that it would be all right. I wanted her to hear that she would be fine wherever she goes. She has friends, angels and good spirits. She had many more friends out there than here on earth. She was welcomed wherever she goes, that there will be a party for her, and she will be blessed and in bliss... I wish that I could have said to her that, as much of a fighter she was, that the battle was not hers to fight. It was not hers to determine how, nor when.

As much of a fighter that she was, I wish she knew when to throw down the towel and accept what the Lord had judged for her. It would have eased her suffering a bit to lay down arms and accept the ultimate judgment. Surrender was often a theme that she and I talked about, about what it says in my religion, Islam, which means "to surrender." I know that deep in her heart, in the core of her being she understood all of these things, but kept it a secret from us all, myself included. This is also a source of pain, to realize that as close to her as I am and had been, she would still not include me in some of her intimate and closely held secrets. I realize however that with love and understanding I must let it be. One should not be so selfish, controlling, or possessive over another to try to be in on all of their matters. An amount of privacy and distance should always be observed. My beloved knew this well, and oh boy, did she ever practice it. To this day, I am still not able to locate keys for boxes for some of her belongings. I still do not know what's inside them. There are writings and messages that I am not able to decipher in her diaries. There are matters and things that she never spoke to me about. One example is a couple of dolls, legitimate antiques, and I am not aware of their story, nor do I know how to dispose of them. I am going to be patient and wait for a message from her; I am confident that I will hear one in time.

Another question I am toiling with is: what amount of pain does it take to hold things inside the soul while suffering all along, and not revealing it to anyone? I feel that is what my beloved was going through. It hurts; I knew and felt it from her. She spoke of it at times, but I am confident that she was only talking of the physical pain, not the real pain tucked deep inside her soul. The pain over the years in relationships or lack thereof. The pain of being alone in the world in her fight against the monster that was eating away at her every day, faced with the horrible fate that awaited her at the turn of the corner. The pain from having come into the world alone and thrown in the arms of strangers. The pain from having to leave the world not in total closure with that world she had to endure. The pain from having been unable to solve the puzzle of her body and soul, and how they related to the people who raised her, not having had the opportunity to connect with her biological parents. So many unanswered questions! Do we ever hear all the answers here on earth? I reckon not.

I really wanted to hear it from her so that I may have given her some compassionate words of support. Perhaps she knew my response in advance and did not want to hear. As she often put it: "I am only telling you so that you listen; I do not want you to give me a solution." Yet I still wished to hold her hand, and to hug her, and say, "It is alright honey, you will get well and will be taken care of. You are a wonderful and very special being to me, to your friends and family, and to all humanity. The dear Lord would never punish you, nonsense! You are a wonderful creation of his, and you shall dwell in the best he has to offer in the gardens of Eden. You have had a wonderful, full and meaningful life. You have achieved in a short time what many hadn't in a lifetime. You have lived the lives of a student, a caregiver, a Nurse, an investor, an interior designer and builder...all and more, but most of all, you have been an exceptional wife to me. I could not have dreamed of anyone that could possibly fill your shoes. For this, I am forever thankful. Even if I had to live one more day only, I have already had the best that life had to give, from you. I am satisfied and pleased; it matters not anymore if I lived longer. My years with you were a good life; everything after is a mere survival."

May 1, 2007

Today I happen to be in the Washington DC area. It seems strange that only one year ago I was here while Mary was in the Orlando area. I was going through one of my difficult times at work, and yet, both of us found a way to deal with the separation that came with the difficulty. I was able to travel back and forth and spend some time with my beloved. She was in great spirits at this time since she had a glimmer of hope that the disease may have been defeated. She had recovered with flying colors from a couple of rounds of Chemotherapy, a Mastectomy and radiation back to back. We had great hopes that these bad episodes of pain, anxiety and fear were behind us. She seemed to be well under way healing herself. She started a new diet; she ate healthier and was walking, despite the pain. She had the love of living and the untamed heart of a fighter, and she was preparing to go on her lifelong dream of visiting Italy. Everything seemed right and ripe. Destiny had it that her malaise, fears and sickness all came back at once during the trip to Italy. She would never recover from that episode which led to her death on the twelfth day of January.

So why am I still struggling? I think that I have rationalized it all, understood it all, given it all to God and came to grips with it. The Counselor says that I am doing well and that I present all healthy symptoms of grief and the healing journey, and I am taking care of myself, although I haven't had much of an appetite lately. I'm left with the question: why?

I realize that there are some things that I have not completely come to grips with. I am still not finding closure due to the fact that we really did not have "real" discussions in her later days. I feel as though I was robbed from having those discussions when that they mattered most, when time was dwindling fast and not to be had ever again. Why?

Why? I mentioned earlier that, at the end, I wanted to convince her that it was all right if she did not live more. I wanted to hear her say it with me because I know she knew that her life on earth was indeed counted in days and hours at the time. I knew she knew, but did not talk. I curse the medicine and the doctors, because they kept her so drugged up that she no longer was conscious enough to talk (I would not say *hear* or *feel*, because she was undoubtedly capable of that.)

I also wished she had told me or wrote to me what her last wishes were. There are numerous artifacts, personal things from her childhood, nice and valuable effects that I am sure she would have loved to give to some close friends or relatives. For the most part we had a clear understanding about these things. We had a Last Will & Testament drawn and signed. We had a mutual agreement on how her major assets were to be disposed of. But I do not know what she wanted to do with her precious and personal items. I can only guess, based on her life, her friendships and hints that she dropped here and there.

It is a very hard thing to do. When I was disposing of some of her stuff last weekend with the girls, there were some of the things where we simply decided to wait and see. I will pray on them and hope that her living and strong spirit will present itself with the right choice. Knowing Mary, this shouldn't be hard. I know

I am connected with her and that, whatever I will do, it will certainly be in her honor and with her spirit present in mind. I am only motivated by good deeds that will, in turn, become good prayers and supplication for her. Those are the things that she will take with her to the hereafter regardless of what people may or may not want, and regardless of if the appropriate thing is done with her belongings.

As a simple example, when I took some her belongings to the shelter for abused women, I knew in my heart that this is something that my beloved MK would be supportive of. I knew that she herself had donated to this cause; I knew in my heart that this was the right thing to do. I think that it is even more worthy of a cause than giving to a close relative or friend. So this would be the driving force, idea and litmus test for any other course of action I follow with regards to her stuff. God as my witness, and her spirit too, I still pray that I will do the right thing in the end!

May 5, 2007

I am at my usual spot at Panera, and a stream of thoughts, emotions, reminiscence and memories flow in at once. As I was having dinner with Rose, MK's cousin, I got teary eyed thinking about the times when we all, including MK, would cook and eat dinner over a glass of wine and enjoy Rose's dry sense of humor. Rose is awesome, although not an expressive person when it comes to showing emotion or talking about the matter, like the emotions evoked by memory of MK. But she was, and still is, there for me.

She listens often without saying anything. But her silence speaks volumes of how she feels: the sorrow, the sadness and the void of her beloved cousin. She loved her very much and I know that. Rose used to stay with my beloved MK when I was out of town. She consoled her when she felt lonely or when the pains and torment of cancer became too much to handle. As my beloved used to say, Rose would express her emotions too much, give you mysterious looks, tell jokes, or talk for hours about nothing, but all along she was saying that she cared, she loved, and that she was touched. After the passing of MK Rose kept the tradition alive. She still comes in the house when I am traveling on the road as it were. She feeds the cat, cooks a meal, cleans the house and does whatever that is needed to be done. She acts as if things haven't changed at all, as if time had not passed since she started coming to the house a couple of years ago. She gives me great comfort just to have around, as we talk and shed tears in memory of the old days.

She came over yesterday and we each had a hot plate of her spaghetti with special sauce, basil, onions and lots of garlic. I was thinking about MK, and I invoked her presence and made a toast to her memory. I cannot help it, every situation, place or person either reminds me of MK or her absence. She was there with me whenever we met with friends and family, whether it was a party, a simple meal or just a drink. Everything I did she was present in it, she partook in everything. She was my friend, and my only friend.

That is probably the hardest thing to adjust to. We would take walks around the lake in our neighborhood, we would eat out around town, and we went on trips together. I did all these things almost exclusively with her. How am I to replace her or look for someone with which to share such a wide variety and range of things and activities? She was a friend for everything and anything, even when I talked about topics that are dear to me, or at least are exciting for me to talk about, such as politics, health issues and religion. She was my discussion partner and would often take the opposite side. She enjoyed pretty much the same things I did. She was a true friend indeed.

May 15, 2007

Another daunting task was awaiting me this week as I took a break from travel to tend to matters at home. I wanted to clear up some of my beloved MK's stuff. It was paperwork this time as opposed to clothing items, which I sorted out last week. This might have been just as hard. In fact, it was even harder. There were many personal things among the papers, and some of them were written in her handwriting.

I was struggling to hold my errant thoughts and tears back. I yelled at myself to stop. I must realize that whatever I am feeling at the moment, I have felt before, that the tears that I shed in the past were for the same reasons. That there is no reason to take myself though that torment again and again. I guess I am telling myself to face the fact that things will not change, that the fact is my beloved MK is gone, and no amount of pain, sorrow or tears can bring her back, and it won't make me feel any better either. I need to move on.

My last visit to the grave site was interesting. I did not have my Quran with me so I played it on my phone. I have a couple of verses stored there that I listen to sometimes, especially when driving far distances. This really saved the day when I found I didn't have my paper copy. But the best part was when I laid down on the grave site beside MK's head and listened to the verse. It felt great as I was lying down next to her. What a wonderful feeling to be next to the one you love, although in this case I could only be with my beloved in memory.

May 29, 2007

Today was Memorial Day. I spent a part of it at the house of Mary Barbara, MK's cousin, who as always was very generous and gracious with the family's traditional cook-out. I would have been there with Mary.

Last week I had donated some of Mary's personal stuff to the Library at the Cancer Center wing of the Orlando Regional Medical Facility, where my beloved had spent most of her days since her cancer diagnosis.

During this past painful season MK had amassed quite an arsenal of medical knowledge, anything having to do with a cure for cancer. She had acquired all sorts of research papers about it, information on the proper nutrition combat it, and had even practiced non-medical things such as yoga, to relax and improve her chances. She even researched biblical teachings that dealt with the power of love and prayer in the search for cure. She lived and breathed the disease all the time. She read numerous books on the subject: *Curing Cancer with Nutrition*, *The Maker's Diet* and *The Purpose Driven Life,* to name a few. Her sense of dedication and combative spirit were unequaled. She amazed me with her efforts. She was passionate about health and possible cures even to her dying days. I felt that her tremendous efforts and research, her personal insights into the disease process, and her powerful thoughts and spirituality were every bit an encouragement, a guiding light and a model to follow. I felt that her story had to be told so that it may bring encouragement and hope to others. I wanted so much to share all of it with others, especially with those who are struggling with the disease.

This is why I have donated all of these materials, including her books and her personal journal, to the library at ORMC. The people there, volunteers and librarians, felt the same passion about the idea, as well as the good spirit of my beloved MK. They could not help but realize that they were in the presence of a real warm spirit as they listened to Mary's story. It felt great to do something so good, and I am delivered a bit more from the painful memory.

I also received a promise from the Volunteers Program Director that there will be a dedication to Mary as part of having her books available to others to read at the library. This shall insure that her spirit will live on, her name would not be forgotten, and her legacy will remain strong and enduring.

May 30, 2007

Next weekend, Mary's mother will be holding a special ceremony to mark her passing. I will not be attending. I still cannot come to grips with her family. I am on bad terms with MK's mother in particular. She has not been supportive throughout this ordeal. She has never volunteered a phone call to express sympathies, see how I am doing or even say a kind word. She is as distant now as when MK was alive. As far as I am concerned, I lost her friendship, her kinship when I lost MK. She wanted me to call her a mother at some point, but that will never happen. Besides that, I think ceremonies are just drama for its own sake. If they truly want to do something in Mary's honor, then let it be some altruistic activity. It could be anything: donating to charity, doing some volunteer work in her honor, or coming to my house and helping me sort through MK's belongings. I could use the help, and it concerns the whole family, but we have always been out of touch when it came to priorities.

But it is all in the past now, and I have to grow past it and realize that we are all accountable only to the Lord for what we do or say. As far as I am concerned, I have already shared the best of what that family had to offer. Her name is Mary Kathryn, and after that nothing else really matters. I give them all peace and I shall move on.

I am still thinking about the visit to the Cancer Center library. That was really soothing for me. I am always charged with positive energy when I am doing something to honor my beloved MK, and am keeping her name and legacy alive. I feel good when I do what she would have done. I also feel some relief from survivor's guilt. I still don't think I feel complete closure, that I have done all I could, that I have honored my MK as she deserves, or that I have always been good to her. I am not sure that I was always as fair, kind and loving as she was to me. I could never be that even if I had lived another hundred years.

It is impossible to equal her kindness and love. I can only hope that I am able in some small way to continue the good she used to do. This is no small task. Giving away her belongings and organizing events honoring what she stood for, these all are ways in which I'd like to redeem myself for how I failed in our relationship. Maybe I am trying to make up for the time we can no longer have together by bringing our relationship to maturity. By doing all of these things alone, I am trying to catch up with her in pleasing the Lord, which is something that MK believed in very openly. I am trying to please the Lord in the way I understand it, and I hope I am correct about it. I am trying to make sure that she still receives the prayers that the Lord counts in the balance of good deeds for her.

In my belief system, a man or woman, after they pass on, can no longer change anything in how their journey in the hereafter will be. It has been sealed through the way they have lived their lives, how they treated others and how devout to the Lord they were. Devoutness not only has to do with ritual and worship, but also in the way they conduct themselves and take advantage of God's bestowed gifts of life, health and all material things on earth. Once they are in the eternal resting place all that matters are the good prayers that others, loved ones as well as strangers, make in their honor. They then become dwellers in Eden, and their resting place is like a morsel of paradise where they may be free to find eternal happiness. The soul of the dead is able to fly high and free, to meet whomever it wants, both loved ones who have passed and whomever else, free and forever. That is wonderful, and the ultimate accomplishment.

My beloved MK has certainly achieved a higher level of spirituality, religious devoutness, and reached the purest form of mankind, that which is most desirable to the Lord. She shall therefore dwell in paradise. Perhaps she is already counted amongst the angels, who are trusted to carry on the message of mercy and love to whomever the Lord wishes to send. She was a messenger of love and kindness already when she was on earth; for this task she needs no training. She has long experience in this subject. I just wish I were one of the chosen recipients of her love and kindness. I trust I am.

June 1, 2007

Once again I am at Panera's enjoying a cup of coffee. I am out of the house because Angie, a tenant at the winter Park house, is cleaning it. Angie is a cancer survivor, and shared many of her experiences with my beloved MK. MK used to give her advice and guided her through many struggles, so Angie is still very fond of MK, and often speaks kindly of her. She often likes to stop by the house and do chores like cleaning. She made a very nice garden in the front yard in memory of MK. There was an iron heart-shaped rod, and Angie planted some pretty flowers at its base. Now they have grown, and they cover the whole heart. It is a wonderful tribute.

My beloved MK touched so many lives. There were no random, passing or unimportant people in her life. Everyone she met meant something to her. She was genuinely interested in people, in their lives, their sorrows and their joys. She could meet a person for just a minute but she would care enough to get their name and number, and would promise to call. She could run into someone and immediately find something kind to say about them.

Once she saw a lady walking down the street not far from the hospital where she was being treated. She was elderly and accompanied by a young boy, so Mary stopped and offered them a ride. After striking up a conversation, she discovered that the old lady was the boy's grandmother. He had lost his parents, and the grandmother was his sole caregiver. The woman was also sick and pursuing treatment at the hospital, and was obviously poor to the point that she could not afford to leave the young boy at daycare. The boy was hungry, and said to his grandma that there was not enough satisfactory food in the house, that there was spaghetti but no meat. MK was so touched by the scene that she offered to take them to eat at a place of their choice. The grandmother was touched but did not want to impose and kindly declined. But MK insisted, especially when the kid excitedly said he hadn't been to McDonald's in a while. Finally, the grandmother accepted the invitation and on they went to McDonald's.

June 23, 2007

It is the day before I fly out to Morocco for some much needed R&R. I would have loved to have my beloved come along.

The last time MK and I went home was in the summer of 2004. We had a great time with the family. MK as usual was involved in all facets of our lives. She cooked, she talked (or tried to) with family members, and she got interested in our culture. She was always looking for ways to immerse herself in Moroccan life, not just to please and get closer to me and my family but for her own edification. She did so brilliantly. I will miss her in Morocco as well.

August 4, 2007

I came back from Morocco last week and I am still under the hypnotic effect of being in the company of family, friends and loved ones, as if nothing had happened all these years that I have been gone. It was as if time had stood still all this time. It is a wonderful feeling to be loved unconditionally, to let your guard down and soak it all up, to plunge back in time into wonderful youth memories, to fall back into that unique place among your own people. As a friend put it, when amongst family, everyone occupies a certain role, and no matter how long you have been away and whatever has happened to you, when you are back amongst family, you fall immediately and automatically into that role. It is amazing how effortless it is.

We shared so much during this vacation. My brothers, sisters and parents all expressed their feelings about MK's passing. It hit them hard as we remembered when she had visited in the past. We laughed at some of the memories, but we also cried quite a bit too. We cried over the fact that she was so instrumental in getting the new family house in Casablanca, yet she would never have the chance to see it. We laughed over the time she mimicked members of the family, which brought everyone onto their bellies in laughter. We laughed at the memory of her teaching Hicham, my younger brother, English, whilst giving him treats like a puppy when he got an answer right. We laughed at the time when she got bogged down by street vendors and answered in Moroccan dialect with her American accent to say "No, it is enough, go away!!"-- the Vendors dropped their mouths from surprise. One of them said "I swear to Allah, I would have never thought she would be Moroccan." That's my Mary; wherever she went she made an impression.

There were many incredible moments during the vacation, but the most amazing of them were the visions that Mom and my brother Ali had of Mary. Mom adored MK and vice-versa. They were very close and shared a deep connection, and incredible powers to heal and see through souls. They felt it around each other. Ali too felt a connection with MK. He says that often sees her in his dreams, including the one I told you about before.

Mom dreamed recently that she was at the house and suddenly felt that someone was coming home, and was about to knock at the door. She leaned forward from the window to look outside and MK was coming towards the house wearing a green ankle long garment. (She did in fact have one of those, given to her by Mom.) But the most intriguing thing was the fact that she balancing an oven board over her head.

In Morocco, back before people had ovens inside the house, and even now on special occasions when baking something big, housewives would make dough and send it out to the baker to bake. The baker is usually coupled with the Hammam (or Turkish bath) because both use wood to heat up a brick oven, so it serves two purposes: the oven heats food for the baker and water for the Hammam.

In Mom's dream, MK was walking comfortably while balancing the board that contains five freshly baked round pieces of Moroccan bread. Mom, in her dream, thought to herself "What does Mary know about Moroccan bread? How did she get it? How can she manage to carry on her head without dropping it?" Of course, as we discussed amongst the family when Mom recounted the dream, there was deep meaning in the story. It is a message from God, or maybe even a message from Mary herself. The fact that MK was wearing green was interesting, as it is a symbol of Islam as the prophet–praise be upon him–was known to wear a green outfit or headpiece. The five baked pieces of bread are seen as symbol for the five pillars of Islam. So, as Mom and I interpreted it, MK was able to balance the Islam faith although it is foreign to her and despite the fact that she was not knowledgeable in the religion.

As I mentioned it earlier, Mary did confess her faith as Muslim, and read quite a bit of the Quran despite the fact that her beliefs encompassed all religions, including some far eastern beliefs. In our faith Islam, only one's self and the Lord truly know one's intent, and what lies deep in their heart. So if this is a message from the Lord, it confirms to us that she truly felt Islam in her heart and accepted it as her religion in the end as she was leaving this world. It is also a confirmation to me at least that I have done the right thing by burying her in the Islamic way and sending her off with Islam as her salvation and the way she will meet her Maker and meet me in the hereafter when we see each other again.

I am not making a self-righteous statement here. I am looking for a sign that what I have done was correct, that what I have felt about her passing and the way she parted with earth was correct. I felt so strongly about her going into the Islamic faith because it was, according to my faith, the only way our souls could join each other, in a blessed, unified way and in keeping with God's commands. I have also been mindful, to a degree, about the way others, especially her closest family members and friends, would feel about the issue. I had been concerned, in my heart and mind, the most with how she would want to go, but it would be an added satisfaction if all her family and friends felt that way too. I guess that this dream answered part of the question. I feel so good and peaceful about that.

Ali also had an incredible dream: He dreamed that my late brother Hassan, who passed in July of 2004 from a brain Aneurysm and meningitis, was coming home. MK was also coming, and they are meeting in the house. But Ali, in the dream, did not understand why I was coming home too, and carrying a big heavy bag on my back. He was thinking that there was no need for it, that I could have sent it with MK or not even have brought anything with me at all.

As we talked about at home, we came up with a plausible explanation. Of course such explanations are not scientific, and are heavily subjective. Does the dream bring happy thoughts and feelings, or are they worrisome and perturbing? In our case, the dreams are beautiful, happy and positive. They give me a great sense of satisfaction and inner peace.

Hassan and MK, two dead people, are meeting. This is great. In our belief system, the dead, if blessed and faithful, shall be able to visit whom and wherever they want. The two of them to be coming home is symbolic of closure, peace and a return to rest. This too is great. As for me carrying a big weight that I am bringing home, it symbolizes one of two things. I feel that the first is correct, at least I hope that it is.

I am bringing a weight back home. It symbolizes that I am finally bringing my sorrow, sadness and misery from the passing of MK back home to share with the family, to be healed by them, for them to give the support and love which ought to get me through it. I am also making peace with the passing of both Hassan and MK; not only that, but I am also able to meet them on a metaphysical level, and am able to connect with them. They are also able to help with the load, because they are at home where I am bringing it.

Another explanation could be that I am ready to move on to the hereafter and the realm of spirit, and so to meet Hassan and MK who have made the crossover before. This also explains the fact that I am coming home and getting rid of the heavy burden of life. I do not think that this was the fact since I am already back in the US, alive and well. Praise be to Allah.

I have met a girl named Tamara. She is wonderful, and a great "Karma girl" as people call her. She is very positive, caring and loving. I needed someone, and she came at the right time. We had no real plan made, but we have known each other nearly a couple of months now, and we feel so close. Does it mean that it was meant to be? I hope so. She has been a great addition in my life and it feels great to be around her. Such interesting things occurred in the month that I was away in Morocco.

October 5, 2007

This weekend, Tamara and I went to Tallahassee, in Florida. This is another stop in my healing journey, which I have postponed for some time. Before, I could not gather the necessary strength to make the trip.

Tallahassee holds a special place for me. This is where Mary and I had spent many years in the 90s going to school. This is also where some of our school friends live. The last time I was there was in the company of my beloved. I did not know how to make the trip on my own or how to face my Tallahassee friends by myself, because every time I had been there Mary was always by my side. I am glad that Tamara was with me. I probably wouldn't have mustered the strength to do it alone.

In the summer of 2005, shortly after Mary was diagnosed with cancer, the Tallahassee crowd, as we knew them, held a special party for us, by the side of the pool at a friend's parents. They wanted to party and laugh in the face of the threatening and brutal disease that is cancer.

In the beginning of the struggle Mary and I made a pact that this would be a new beginning, not an end. It would be another chance to live: cleaner, better and much stronger. In that same spirit, the Tallahassee crowd wanted to celebrate Mary's life and will to live. That weekend, the whole gang decided to all cut their hair in honor of Mary. It was a known fact that she was going to lose her hair very soon from chemotherapy. This was not an easy thing for Mary to bear, for she had gorgeous blond and curly hair. Everybody loved it and complemented her on it. Rather than losing it gradually, Mary decided to cut it real short and donate the cuttings to the charity "Locks of Love," who collect and create wigs which are then donated to sick children suffering from terminal diseases.

As a gesture of solidarity, we all decided to cut our hair with Mary. Robert, a practicing attorney, shaved his head completely even though looks are important to his profession. He was fresh out of law school and new to his work, making the choice no easy matter. One of our gang was a lady in her late fifties who had never cut her hair until then, but she joined in. What they did for her spoke volumes of the kind of emotion, sacrifice, love and humanity displayed by any genuine human beings. Dawn, her mother Kathy, her husband Scott, her two beautiful children Todd and Kaitlyn, Robert, his family; and myself, we all decided to cut their hair short or altogether going bald! We called the event the "Hair Cutting Party." We were overwhelmed and overcome with emotion, of all sorts: sadness coupled with happiness, grief combined with joy.

I realized then that these people, despite their different backgrounds, all loved Mary, and recognized her as the great person she was. She was a true friend to all and each one of them. They all had a story to tell, an incident where Mary showed them love and support. Robert did not know her too well, but there was something about Mary that drew him into her. Teary eyed and sobbing, he said "I don't how I can explain this, but I often think about Mary and I cry. She is just special. She is one of those people that when you meet them, you say to yourself, I do not know why, but I love this person, I am drawn to her."

The visit was a great success, and everybody gathered to tell stories from the past. Sometimes tears fell uncontrollably and other times laughs were unstoppable. Emotions were mixed. Everyone expressed their approval of Tamara. She is kind, friendly and very outgoing. She is, therefore, right in place with the Tallahassee crowd. They were also so pleased that I finally decided to come up. They were fearful that they would lose me after Mary's passing. As it often happens in similar situations, parties part ways if the central person, the glue that brings them together, disappears. Mary was just such a person: a bridge builder, a force for positivity, a healer and mediator.

I felt much better after the trip. I knew I still had a family of sorts in Tallahassee. I am connected to these people forever; they were part of my past. Now and forever, they are part of my present and future. They remind me of good old days, of happy times of youth and carelessness during the college years of early 90's. They will always play the role of that bridge to my past in Tallahassee. They are a constant reminder that the spirit of Mary still lives on; her legacy always carries on since they are, by default or unseen design the protectors of Mary's story in Tallahassee. Indeed, she had quite a life in Tallahassee. She was working at the homeless shelter to feed the poor and homeless in the area. She even helped out with stray and abused animals.

She also played a major part in bringing down a bastion of ignorance, bigotry and racism that plagued those parts, the Nicholson's Farm House. For a time, Mary worked hard at this awful place, and was victim of their shameful, archaic and unlawful practices. This would be a story to tell in the future, but the bottom line is that the restaurant was brought to court, and their manager and owners forced to admit wrongdoing and pay restitution. The restaurant closed its doors, putting an end to bad chapter in the history of the area. Mary was the one who instigated the law case and brought the restaurant to justice when all other sat around and watched. The Farm House was an institution in the area, deeply rooted in the past and well connected to the point that no one believed it was possible to bring them down, let alone a woman. But Mary wasn't just any other female; she was a strong woman, fearless and determined to get justice served. God bless her spirit.

In the times of trials and testing that the almighty blesses us with, sometimes the best of human character rises to the surface. Clearly such a thing happened in Tallahassee. Mary Kathryn's friends all rose to the occasion for a show of utmost love, compassion and solidarity. It was not Mary Kathryn's persuasion skills that made them friends, nor was it the sorrow they felt for her condition, it was something greater. It was the Lord's awesome magic and power that created a moment of bliss, within which all could discard their inhibitions, selfishness and fear, and embrace the Lord's gift of love, compassion and strength within all of us. These people, forever and as long as they live, have etched a single divine moment when they all, at once and equally, felt empowered by God to stand in solidarity and love. It demonstrated the close, intimate and sincere friendship they all share with Mary Kathryn. She has touched their lives and vice-versa. May we all be blessed and privileged to have such good friends that one need not to say anything to them, but yet, by divine instinct, their hearts, minds and souls know what needs to happen.

God bless all.

October 22, 2007

Yesterday was an amazing day. It was the culmination of a celebration. I participated in the 3-Day Breast Cancer Walk held in Tampa, FL.

Words cannot begin to explain how I felt. I was overwhelmed and in utter shock and awe. I was lifted up to a higher state of awareness. Even though as a support volunteer I only participated in a portion of the walk on the last day in support of our friend, Carol Ann, I felt the energy immensely. Carol had been Mary's dearest friend in Tampa, and she made a promise to Mary while she was still alive that she would walk in her honor. As Carol Ann recounted the story on Sunday after the walk and we were lounging in her patio, exhausted physically and emotionally after the walk, she said that she did not really know what to offer Mary for her birthday when she was really ill last year. She explained in her own words "What can you possibly offer? What things can you possibly buy for someone who is struggling to stay alive?" The only thing that came to her mind at the time was the Breast Cancer Walk. It was just about the same time as the Susan G. Komen walk was held in Tampa. Carol had just witnessed the event since much of the walk and the subsequent closing ceremony take place in her neighborhood. She was inspired to walk in honor of Mary. Little did she know that she would expire less than three months later.

Carol kept her promise, and in doing so, inspired us all to be there and share in the moment. My girlfriend Tamara and Mary's close friend Barbara came for the walk too. But Carol was supposed to have a whole team walking with her. We had planned to have a whole team walking in Mary Kathryn's honor. It was to be named *Bubbles of Love* in her honor, for Mary used to finish all of her letters, postcards and emails with the words "Bubbles of Love." She would also blow kisses for good byes and say "bubbles of love!" at the same time. I had shirts especially made for the occasion, which we wore during the event, depicting bubbles in blue and violet, with one bubble showing a picture of Mary with short hair after chemotherapy at the time of the picture, and with "Bubbles of Love" printed on the shirt.

Mary's cousin Mary Barbara was also supposed to walk, but could not due to recent foot surgery, which pretty much took her out of any strenuous physical activity. A couple of Carol's friends filled in the missing initial team members, and they all trained and walked together in Mary's honor.

The first day, a Friday, was awful, and it was too hot and muggy to do much walking. Carol had to cut her walk short of the twenty miles, but still managed to make it for fifteen miles, which all considered is still a big accomplishment. Many of the others had to call the walk off half-way.

The second day much smoother, and the weather was much better. Carol Ann then went the entire second segment, twenty miles in all. She was great! The atmosphere was contagious, especially when the last walker made it to camp at about five PM, which would have been a grueling seven-hour day spent walking, not an easy feat by any measure. But we didn't care about the time, this was exactly the spirit of solidarity, sisterhood and compassion the event was all about. Everybody cheered in a sister, friend, or courageous soul who challenged the odds to completed the walk no matter how demanding and emotionally draining it was. When someone made it back to camp, everyone stopped what they were doing to rise and cheer, clap and yell as hard as possible in celebrate the return of the walker. No one could claim victory alone; it was a win for everyone. It was so inspiring that I was brought to tears, and so were many others.

The third day, at the break of dawn, we were all up and ready to walk. We had decided the day before that we were going to wear the Bubbles of Love tee-shirts and walk with Carol to support her, and to call on the beautiful spirit of Mary to join us. Although we, as in Barbara, Tamara and I, were not registered Walkers, we felt it was our duty, that we were called to walk that day. Perhaps the spirit of Mary was calling us to come out and join the crowd. So we "saddled up," and headed out to camp.

The atmosphere was grand and the air was thick with emotion, filled with love and joy. Before sunrise everybody had risen from their tents, and we were all anxious to start the day and walk the final 20 miles. "Good mornings" and cheers were heard everywhere one walked. People were upbeat, smiling and encouraging one another on their way. Some men there were decked out in pink dresses and bras to support the walkers and help them forget about the pains of the day ahead, while others took pictures and laughed. The spirit was contagious, and we could not wait until we got started.

Sixteen miles were ahead of us. People, cars, bike and motorbikes all lined up on the route to cheer the walkers on, decorated for the occasion. Cars and vans were painted with signs such as "You go Girls!" "Way to Go," and other messages of support and love for walking partners and friends.

Some carried messages and pictures in memory of loved ones who had passed from the disease. That was our case with the "Bubbles of Love" message on our shirts. Walkers behind us stopped in their tracks to inquire about the picture and the message on them. I explained the story to few walkers, and some of them wept to hear. One woman, with tears in her eyes, said "I feel the spirit of Mary around. She is walking with you right now." We all cried at this.

Halfway through the sun was high overheard and it was getting hot, but our spirits neither withered nor waned. We kept on, cheering, laughing and chanting. At every rest stop or pit station, walkers stretched, drunk and relieved themselves, but continued on. On two occasions, elderly and tired walkers had to stop on their way and, tired, exhausted or even emotionally drained, were picked up by emergency vehicles. Regardless, everyone stopped in their strides to recognize them, cheer them on and clapped to show support for their effort. No matter how far along they got, their intent was pure and solid. They gave it all and stopped when they run out. They shall receive their rewards too.

The end of the day and the closing ceremony were magical. When you see a sea of pink walking and gathering in one place, you cannot help but be overwhelmed with emotion. I felt the spirit of Mary there with me. I knew that this was the kind of place for her. This is where the group energy that she thrives on would have been for her to enjoy. I could not help but feel sad that she did not get the opportunity to participate in the walk in the physical form. She was an avid walker and had walked the Relay for Life once in life, and was always supportive of woman's issues. Of course she was there. It was meant to be. That is the easiest answer yet the least satisfying of all.

I wondered for a moment why some have second chances and some do not? Why couldn't Mary be here? This was, after all, her place to be. She was, in my mind, more deserving than me, and perhaps more than many participating walkers to be there. So, why? My God, she had so much living in her, so much more to give, so much energy, and she wanted so much to live and defy all the odds stacked against her. Yet it was not to be. It was not her time to go on and be with us, here at the walk. As I see it, she simply had run out of time here on earth. I must accept this explanation, no other is satisfying or makes any sense.

I saw the walkers go the final mile towards the stage to tell their story and that of their respective teams. The story of why they joined, who they were walking for, and what it had meant to them. I also saw the Survivors group, small in numbers, but nonetheless there were a few hundred. I was happy for them; they were the lucky ones, blessed or simply stronger in their genes and their will to live, but still a reminder to how devastating the disease is.

I am praying that their numbers will grow further, year after year. Perhaps the victory of others over the disease is somewhat of a consolation for those of us who were unable to do it for our loved ones or us. We all win if strides are made, if science and love are able to conquer the disease. It is a win for all when growing numbers show up every year, and more cities join the walk to support the sick and the dying. Their defiant spirit is contagious. If my beloved Mary died in the struggle while others in the future are able to survive, then the effort is worthwhile. My walk is therefore for all others who still have a chance to make it. It is worth it if an avenue of research is successful, or if an additional supporting law is enacted, or even if one an additional dollar is raised. Perhaps this effort will help generations to come to conquer the disease. I will make sure that this walk is a tradition of mine, a part of my daily struggle, a part of my reason for being (in the absence of my beloved Mary), and part of what I stand for henceforth, so help me God.

November 10, 2007

Tomorrow, I will participate in a 10K race. I know that 10K is not a whole lot, and I have run further in the past. This time, I am running in memory of my beloved Mary. MK always encouraged me to do so. We had our first run together (she walked mostly) for the Joy of Parenthood race in April 2006. Since then she has always encouraged me, and she was instrumental in making me realize the benefits of running.

She used to work for the Celebration Hospital. She loved what it stood for and the quality of care it provides. Her employment there was supposed to be the culmination of her studies and training, the aim of her graduation from the Nursing program. She wanted to be associated with a great place to work and the sense of care and professionalism that Celebration Hospital is known for. The whole Celebration community is an example of a successful and thriving integrated community. It has earned the praise and admiration of many.

No Way to Treat the Dying

Jan 26, 2008 10:46 AM EST, Newsweek. By Jerry Adler.

Cancer, says Barrett, is 'a fertile field for exploitation because patients are so often frightened.'

What price do you put on hope? Is $3,000 a week too much? Said Nedlouf faced that question when his wife, Mary, was diagnosed with an inoperable recurrence of breast cancer in the summer of 2006. It did not at first seem like too much to spend on "bioresonance therapy," "quadrant analysis" and "autosanguis" treatments by Dr. Jarir Nakouzi, a homeopathic physician in Bridgeport, Conn. "Whatever that woman wanted, I would do it," says Nedlouf, a native of Morocco who met Mary at Disney World and lived with her in Orlando. Now, a year after his wife's death, Nedlouf thinks he made a bad deal. "He sold us hope that wasn't there," says Nedlouf, who has filed a complaint against the doctor with the Connecticut Department of Public Health.

But Nakouzi was the only one who was offering hope. By the time Mary saw him—after a double mastectomy, chemotherapy and radiation—her cancer was incurable, according to her oncologist, Dr. Nikita Shah. At that point conventional medicine could offer only a remission that might last years, months—or weeks.

Nakouzi did talk about a cure, according to Said Nedlouf. "He talked about getting to the 'root' of the cancer, and that there could be as many as 20 roots," Nedlouf says. He recalls that Nakouzi took a history that went back to

Mary's early childhood, focusing on emotional traumas and the deaths of people close to her, probed her with electrodes and prescribed a daily regimen of 30 to 40 pills and supplements. "He talked about eating healthy, using the right toothpaste," Nedlouf says, wonderingly. (Nakouzi declined to be interviewed, citing the ongoing investigation. DPH records show no past disciplinary actions against him.) Homeopathy, a longstanding alternative to standard medical practice that appears to be undergoing a revival, is described on Nakouzi's Web site as "based upon the idea of Similia Similibus Curantur (Like cures Like): A pharmacologically active substance ... triggers a series of symptoms. These same symptoms in a sick person can be cured by giving micro doses of this substance." Dr. Jack Killen, acting deputy director of the National Center for Complementary and Alternative Medicine, says homeopathy "goes beyond current understanding of chemistry and physics." He adds: "There is, to my knowledge, no condition for which homeopathy has been proven to be an effective treatment."

But hope, not proof, is what Mary Nedlouf wanted. On a visit, her cousin Mary Maynard expressed concern about her condition. "I am fine," she retorted. "I am being cured." Cancer, says Dr. Stephen Barrett, who runs the Web site Quackwatch.org, is a "fertile field for exploitation, because patients are so often frightened or desperate." By December, Mary's cancer had broken through the chest wall, covering her skin with an oozing sore. The hotel maids refused to touch her sheets, so Said washed them himself. A cancer-weakened vertebra fractured, excruciatingly. Finally Said stepped in.

He called a halt to the treatments, after, he says, running up bills of about $41,000 (most of which he is disputing). When he brought her home, "it was frightening to see her," says Maynard. The sore on her chest was ghastly. She died a few weeks later.

Said Nedlouf doesn't blame Nakouzi for not curing an incurable cancer. He sees now that Mary's will to live may have tipped over into self-delusion. But is she to blame for that? Nakouzi's useless treatments, he says, "robbed me of precious time to console her, to come to closure, to prepare for her departure." And that seems like a high price for hope.

March 15, 2009

The funny thing about grief is that it never completely goes away. Two years have passed, and yet every once in a while I think back on the life and death of my beloved.

Even having remarried more recently, I can never totally forget my past relationship. But regret is one of the most potent and powerful memories. I think back at some of the exchanges I had with Mary. Sometimes I was mean, or unpleasant. Many times I was in the wrong, yet I argued and disagreed with Mary to the point of hurting her emotionally. These memories that are so painful to me.

Often in silence, I ask her for forgiveness. I make a prayer for her soul and look for ways to repent for my sins. I tell myself that in my present and future dealings, especially those with close ones and loved ones, I must always be kind and gentle. I must be forgiving and generous. It pains me to remember the sad moments that plagued our relationships, especially the years of pain and sickness leading to Mary's death. She was so gracious and strong that she would rarely demonstrate or vocalize her pain. Much of the time, I felt she was hurting quietly and secretly. It is painful to me not to have been privy to this secret suffering. I don't know why she acted that way, and it bothers me that I didn't know. I know that we shared so many of the dreadful times she was going through; I was right there with her the whole time. Yet, I am sorry not to have shared the experience to the fullest. Was she trying to spare me some of the burden of her deep suffering? Perhaps she did not feel that I could handle it all. Maybe some parts and expressions of the suffering were simply just too much. I still don't know why. I still remember those moments as if they were only yesterday. Some strong experiences, I believe, stay with us forever.

For example, I remember the time when back in 1981 when I was rejected from the military academy because of a varicose vein. The denial shocked me, a strong and competitive young man at seventeen. To be refused because of a physical impediment. I would have accepted any other reason but health. I felt shamed, like I was less than the others. I lived in fear, rage and confusion for years until I came to the US and saw a different doctor about the diagnosis. The doctor's diagnosis was that a simple case of varicose veins was predominantly a cosmetic issue, if anything. I pity the incompetent nurse or doctor who denied me access to the academy and led me to believe that I was sick.

I wonder what Mary was thinking about while silently suffering inside. She was living in a different, distant world, all alone, even though we were right next to each other. Sometimes we would go to a quiet little park by the water, just the two of us. It was in the middle of the harsh northeastern fall, and in the middle of the week, so there were hardly any people walking around or strolling there.

Mary would sit on a bench, quietly meditating, touching the part of her chest that was affected with the disease. She would sit there for a couple of hours while I sat nearby, or walked around her as if I was an obedient servant watching his queen, or a nurse watching over his patient. Like a faithful dog watching over his master: no words needed to be said. It was clear what was going on but too painful to express in words. One and another knew what was happening, recognized it, yet kept it silent as if it was taboo.

She could barely walk at the end. I did not know how bad her disease was or how much it has taken her over. She was at its mercy. Everything had become painful to do, every task had become a major undertaking. Yet through all of it, she was still strong and proud. She always made sure that her bluffing wasn't discovered. Her façade of the warrior never faded; she was that way even when she lay on her death bed. She fooled me, no doubt. It hit me hard when I realized the degree of her illness. When we finally visited the emergency room at Bridgeport hospital, the doctor simply said that I should take Mary back home and let her rest.

May 9, 2009

After midnight. Another sleepless night in Orlando at the Palmer Street house, but this night has special significance. It is perhaps the last night I spend here. I am finally renting out the house. A final letting-go of a place that has so many memories for me. I still think of the house as Mary's. It has always been hers and that will never change in my mind.

I was crying last time I was here as I was removing her belongings from the house. I felt that I was symbolically kicking her out. That was when I removed her beautiful wedding gown. It felt like evicting her from the house that she designed, built, loved, and made into a beautiful home for us. But she could no longer stay there, either physically or in spirit. I am sure she found a better home. Wherever she is, it is a better place; she has that skill to make it that.

But here I am going again through that sense of physical separation, this time finally. I am leaving a place where I no longer feel that I belong. It is over and done with. I move on and I bury that memory. I will leave my spirit in that time here, and perhaps she too dwells there forever. It is said that sometimes the spirits of previous residents of a dwelling never leave it, but remain attached to the place, especially if they died there, perhaps as the result of some tragedy. This is at least Mary's case here. I am moving to a different nest that my new wife, Tamara, has made for us at her house in Saint Simons, Georgia.

I am no longer suffering from the feeling of total loss that I had after Mary. None can replace Mary or fill her place in heart. But I have started a new life.

The journey since has become much easier. Life is beautiful once again, with new surprises, new memories, and new things to look forward to. No longer shall I look back and feel total anguish. I see and feel the sadness of what was lost, but also an equal joy and optimism from what I am going through, and what is to come. I am saved, thank the Lord almighty.

So, this is it. I am moving from the house of memories of Mary. I am closing the door on a dear, though sad, chapter of my life. I am physically moving away from the past and saying goodbye, once and for all. The emotions range between sadness from memories of a beautiful house and the person behind it, but also release and relief since no longer shall I feel trapped by the past. I make a distinction here between the beautiful memories that the house holds, and the misery that it has become without Mary.

Good things are coming. Ali gets married on July 11th, and I am entering another marathon. It will be a reality, God willing, and soon.

May 28, 2009

We have been talking about the Dublin, Ireland Marathon recently, and it seems that a bunch of good friends of Tamara and mine are pushing the idea. In my mind, too, it is maturing every day. I am eating well, running, becoming more health conscious. The run will coincide with my birthday week; in fact, it will be just two days before my birthday on the 28th. It will be indeed awesome.

But this is not what I want to write about tonight as I lay sleepless at my friend Chehab's house in Orlando. I want to talk about marital issues.

Tamara and I had a huge fight the night before I left home on Saint Simons Island. This is alarming to me. It is a scary thought to ponder whether a marriage is good, what the future holds for us. Are we going to make it? Are going to grow past our issues?

All pertinent questions, and very difficult to answer. It makes me wonder if we, as partners, are doomed to repeat old mistakes. Are we really so predictable? Can we not change our habits no matter how toxic they may be? It is truly frightening.

I keep falling into the trap of the Ego: the selfish arguments and destructive attitudes I used to have with Mary. It seems that some of the issues that result in our fighting are exactly the same as ones Mary had with me. It is ridiculous that I don't know better after all these years, and with so much more experience. Early in our relationship, Tamara and I that is, I used to worry that, in some respects, Mary may have had a bad deal. But regardless, Tamara would inherit the better, the sweeter and more mature face of me. There is an adage that says we learn much from earlier marriages, to the disadvantage of the previous partner but to the benefit of the new. Perhaps it is a logical and expected progression; we tend to do things better given a second chance. I thought that this would be my case.

But I may have been wrong. It seems that the other adage is more appropriate for me: humans are predictable animals. They act and react in predictable and constant ways no matter the circumstance. We repeat the same behavior as if to say that is who we are, and cannot help but be of that character.

June 20, 2009

This is the first time that I have written from aboard an airplane. It is challenging to keep balance when typing on a small surface. It is a long and painful flight from Atlanta to Las Vegas. It is almost ten p.m., and I have been up since five in the morning. Needless to say I am tired, but I am listening to some good music, the Bombay Dub Orchestra. Just as the name suggests, it is a mix of Hindi music and Reggae dub, which I admit are two of my favorite musical styles. So, I felt inspired to write. It has been a while since I did.

I am headed home and I am once again alone. When Tamara accompanied me this morning to the airport I told her that I was anxious; that I was not totally at ease going home by myself. There are simply way too many thoughts on my mind when I go home. It is a long trip, with at least a couple of stops along the way, and I have to worry about all kinds of logistics concerning tickets, boarding passes, terminals, time changes, and so on. It is a lot to deal with as single person; going as a couple, as we did last year, is much more comforting.

I was listening to some quiet music, the type that makes one reminisce about things, places and all kinds of memories. My mind, as the case often is when I think about the past, tends to drift. That's the person that I am, always thinking about things and seeing more than is apparent.

I was thinking about how in these times of solitude and loneliness I search deep inside myself for strength and guidance. Seldom have I sought the help or advice of others. I go it alone, thinking that I have it all in me to come up with the right answer, believing that I am indeed strong enough to find all I need from within, from the source of energy and strength deep within. When I went through the ordeal of the passing of my beloved, I searched inside, mustered all the strength I had, and told myself that it was do or die, that it was all me, that no one else would be there to guide me through it. No matter what help and comfort others gave, I always felt that I was my best advisor and none else could provide that kind of thing. Deep inside I looked at others with suspicion. I questioned the motives of others and trusted what I felt inside. Perhaps my disappointment in people was so great that I felt that even the ones who have my best interest at heart couldn't be trusted.

But since I am going back home today, it just hit me: why didn't I trust my family? Why didn't I seek help from them? Why didn't I cling to the love that I have for them, and they for me, as source of strength? Clearly my mother would have been supportive, a lamp in the darkness of the journey of my grief. I do not have an answer to this.

All along I have always felt that no matter what relationships and ties I have picked up in my US journey, they couldn't match what I had with my family at home. I was of them, and came from them, and they from me. Words did not have to be spoken for me to know that they felt my pain and joy. They saw my worries and my calm. They saw right through me, without my having to say anything. As a dear friend once said that we in the old Arab world have the knack for hearing what is not said. I think that we, in close families such as ours, have a deep connection with each other, and learn, as we grow together, almost to read each other's thoughts, and react to what we see. We shine at sparing each other's labor, saving them the embarrassment of having to discuss their feelings aloud. Just simply detecting the emotion, the worry and the pain, and reacting to it comfortingly and lovingly, without having to say a word. I don't think the west has learned this type of skill, and they may never indeed.

And yet still, I went at it all alone. I had numerous conversations with Mom as I was going through the ordeal, but I never felt the need to be there with the family, even though I knew comfort was there for me to be had if I wanted it. Instead, I sought strength from inside. I guess I felt that this was a personal struggle I had to emerge from alone. I even found some sort of pride at walking this path alone, as if to demonstrate my utmost love and loss at the same time. What a strange idea!

The journey continues.

November 18, 2009

I ran the Dublin Marathon in a respectable time of four hours and twenty-seven minutes, my personal best. It was thrilling, one of my greatest accomplishments, to be counted among the best one-percent of those who run marathons in the world.

Of course, I thought about beloved Mary as I was running. In part the run was for her. I remember that I told her in 2006, as she was battling her disease, that one day I would run a marathon. I really did not think I could do it then, and didn't treat the idea seriously. But I wanted to sound confident for Mary, for she was very encouraging after she saw how well I ran in the Planned Parenthood 5K.

Halfway through the Marathon run, as fatigue started to set in, I turned to the Moroccan music selection on my iPod for motivation. Out of nowhere came a fast folk song from my Tamazight ancestors. I bawled. I remembered the tune played at the Ifrane Tamazight festival in Morocco in the summer of 2004. Mary and I attended together that year. We were so happy and so full of energy those days. I remember that one evening we danced with a long line of young men emulating the moves of the dancing troop. We laughed and danced till we were exhausted. I had never seen Mary so happy and joyful, just a sight to behold. I thought to myself how awful it was that Mary's journey had to end that way, how sad it was to run with her memory but not her physical presence. So despite my record time, the accomplishment will always remain unfinished to me, and the promise went unfulfilled as one of the promise-makers did not witness it. So sad.

I was crying for the pain she endured as I suffered through my own pain from the long run. I thought to myself, *my pain doesn't even come close to hers*. It is not fathomable how she lived her last agonizing couple of months. Her pain was visible on her face but ran deeper than one could see. Just as a martyr or prophet would suffer for his people to spare them what they couldn't handle, she kept her pain a secret, something that could only be imagined and not truly understood. When she drifted into her own world, holding her hands to her chest, saying a prayer and meditating over her plight, she was quietly suffering. She asked for nothing and wanted nothing. She was not even in this world sometimes. It remained always a puzzling situation how so close I was to her and yet so distant at the same time during those days. She was already on her way out. Another journey had started for her that I could not join her on. I did not know it then but I do now.

So I ran harder and faster with all those memories chasing through my head, as tears ran down my face. I was in such a state that I no longer felt any physical pain at all. I simply ran. I didn't see anyone else around despite the tens of runners nearby and the hundreds of people cheering from the road sides. I was in my own world, alone with memories of Mary. I saw her face, her tears, her sorrows, her suffering, and nothing else.

I then caught sight of a pair of brothers in the race, one running, but pushing the other who was wheelchair-bound. I became even more emotional; I saw there the victory of humankind, an illustration of how the spirit of fraternity and altruism can prevail. Here are two human beings displaying the best of humanity.

How unselfish one can be to help another for no apparent gain. I cried as I thought how I wished I could do this for Mary, if she had lived but was left in a similar state.

I came to mile 18. 1 was supposed to meet a pair of friends, Dawn and Thomas, on the side of the road, and we would finish the race together. More than three hours had passed and there were still eight miles left to go. My friends waiting for me was just the extra push I needed. I was feeling drained and without the strength to finish up. The thought of walking had run through my head several times as we were crossing the twenty-mile mark, but they pushed me to continue my stride and pace to the finish. Tom yelled "Come on Said, you can do it," and "It is done, you are almost there," and "Hang in there buddy, you are doing it," on and on. I was starting to slow down, but they were always there next to me, or just a bit ahead and encouraging me to catch up with them.

At mile twenty-three, when I was nearly spent, Tom reminded me that we were only a measly 5K away from finishing, a distance that I have run many times without a blink. But these were no regular three miles, but the last three miles in a twenty-six mile run, and almost four hours in. I knew I was totally fatigued, mentally and physically, when I thought I saw the mark for twenty-three miles again, as if I had run by the sign twice. But I continued to run, and I shouted to myself, "This one is done, it is in the pocket, and I have finished this run already." And I did.

April 4, 2010

It is the long flight back from Las Vegas again, the sin city of the west as it is known. I am listening to some old Indian classics from Bollywood. They bring back memories from my childhood when we used to go to cheap theaters that played cheap Indian movies that the poor could afford. The melody and stories were very similar to ours; they deal with society's taboos, class struggles, love many issues that the poor had to deal with. It was a way to travel in one's seat to those exotic lands in India and their mysterious ways.

I am thinking back to the Dublin Marathon. I felt suddenly rejuvenated as I approached the last mile, 3300 yards from the goal. I knew then that I was going to finish the race then, and started thinking about the celebration. What would I do, jump from joy, or kiss the ground or bow to the Lord in prayer, or shout out from the depths of my lungs? I was thinking of something dramatic. I had rehearsed so many ways in my head while I was training in the previous few months. When I tired from running I would tell myself, "Just think when you are running for real during the race, how tired will you be then? Think of the finish line, and how great it will feel to finish and how relieved you will feel. How thrilled would you be with that accomplishment!"

I had been telling myself that no matter how hard my preparation runs were, no matter how challenging they were and how tired I felt while running them, I would feel worse pain during the run. But thinking about the end, the thought of the banner reading "FINISH" would make the fatigue disappear at once, and anticipating the feeling of accomplishment and deep satisfaction made all the pain fade away. But when I did cross the finish line, I raised my arms, just smiled, and just continued forward to the water station. I was in so much pain and awe that I had no desire to do anything; I simply continued walking in a daze. I forgot all about how I would celebrate. I was done! I finished! That's all there is to it. Anything else I did no longer mattered, as the important thing was accomplished: to finish.

Even when I saw my friends and Tamara, I was still stunned from the run. They reminded me: "How do you feel?" Tamara yelled, "You did it baby; you ran the Marathon!" Only then did I remember what the accomplishment meant to me, to all my friends and family, and all the discussions we had leading to it. Only then did I realize that I kept my promise. I lived up to the challenge and conquered all the fears and doubts I had about running the Marathon.

It all came back at once. I remembered that, a few years back, when I thought about it I would push it away as impossible. It was just a fleeting dream about what could be possible if I kept running, had the discipline and the drive to continue, stayed healthy and followed a proper regimen. It was crazy for me then to even think that I could consider running the distance. I remembered that MK once told me that I could do it. I had smiled and brushed it aside.

But as time passed, I thought more about running. I had to find somewhere deep inside, something strong enough to push me forward. Mary's death was a catalyst. I began running more, for longer distances, and getting better at timing and effort. I could do it for her. The mere fact that she said, "You can do it baby," was incentive enough to attempt the run at any price. I shouted back. "I did it! I did it! I did it!" The thought after that was, "I do not want to do this again," but what does that matter? I did it once, and I do not care if I ever run again. It was done! The challenge was over.

Or was it? I am thinking about another marathon for 2010. I would like to repeat the feat, and maybe finish in a better time than 4:27. Could I even break four hours? It could be possible for me and for the shape I am in to break that time. We will see.

September 27, 2012

In fact, I did run again, this time in the Walt Disney World Marathon. It was not a sub-four hour run, but I did improve my time to 4:18. It was not too shabby for my old legs.

The run was dedicated to my beloved MK. I ran on the very grounds where I first saw, met, and later married her. Walt Disney World was part of our lives at all of our important junctures, so what a better way to honor all of that, and the life of Mary, than to run the Disney Marathon in her honor.

The day was great, and the run was fun. Mary was on my mind the whole time. I remembered the times we met at each park restaurant, each event where we strolled hand in hand, or ate, or had a moment. There were many such moments, which made my run much easier as my mind constantly drifted way back to these memories, some more than twenty-five years old, others just seven or eight years.

The end of the race was at the EPCOT center park. It was where we met properly for the first time on that lovely spring afternoon in 1988. I remembered vividly every landmark where we walked and talked. Where we had that first beer at the Mexican Cantina, where we visited the Japan Showcase, and so on.

I was awash in memory. I was no longer worried about finishing the race, or about my time, or the mounting pains. It all vanished, and I only saw me and MK strolling in the park.

I caught a glimpse of the announcement that we were nearing the last mile marker. I was almost there.

I started hearing the chants of a gospel band that was placed immediately outside of the American pavilion showcase. I knew then that I was very near the end. MK and I sat outside of the American pavilion to have ice cream on many occasions; it was sometimes the beginning of our walk around the park, or the end of it, depending where we started the tour.

As I was thinking of her, the unbelievable occurred. A number of staff were standing outside the pavilion, wearing their usual uniform in honor of the early settlers of America. They cheered the race participants as they made their last few hundred strides towards the finish line. That is where I caught a glimpse of a smiling face; a tall blondish young girl. She couldn't have been more than 20, with long blond hair, fair skin and beautiful eyes. She was the exact image of my MK!

It happened so quickly. I could not believe my eyes. I wanted to run back and make sure that I saw wasn't a figment of my imagination... but, I did not. I continued to the finish line, and made it.

I have reflected on what I saw. Was I day dreaming? Was my mind wandering in the pain of those last few hundred steps? Were my memories intermingling with my imagination? Or was it perhaps the angel Mary reappearing in the face of a young MK in her twenties, back when I first met her?

It was incredible. I can picture this face even now. I have thought about this a lot as I shared the memory with close friends and relatives, and I still cannot get an answer. I still remember the face. Maybe I should revisit Disney and the American pavilion just to put this at rest.

But why do that? I am satisfied that I saw what I saw, even if it wasn't real. It was real *in the moment.* It looked every bit like it was real to me, and it made me feel what I needed at that time. It was enough.

October 30, 2012

As I review this manuscript for submission, I sitting admiring a picture of two little creatures that are now part of my new life. They are Malak and Kenza, two toddler sisters whom Tamara and I adopted a little over a year ago from Morocco. I have finally realized that dream of parenting that I had considered for years. I refer back to earlier in this writing where I was longing to have children of my own, that I was saddened by the fact that MK did not conceive children. Both of us have always had children in our lives, from close family and friends, and vicariously we have lived the lives of parents through relatives, friends and loved ones. But to have ones that you call your own is certainly another dimension.

But it seemed strange to me, even today, to realize the fact that I am a parent, even if only through adoption. I would have never imagined that in the past I would be traveling a long way to find little angels to adopt. Adoption is not condoned in the Islamic sense. It is called *kafala*, and it is more like a guardianship.

How did it come about? How did this idea grow to become reality? Aunt Joe, who is MK's aunt, is always reminding me that my beloved is looking after me, and not to mistake the fact that her guiding spirit was behind this big accomplishment. I have noticed that their initials spell out *M.K.*

I somehow am blessed again, even after my beloved's passing. I am blessed because I see her spirit working in all that has happened to me since. Her angel is here and looming over all. Malak calls her "Angel Mary" and calls her old plant "Angel Mary Flower." We got another plant for the backyard and also named it "Angel Mary's" Malak loves it and waters it on occasion. Mary's memory is eternal, here to stay after my passing, here to stay in the care of Malak's and Kenza's generation. They will carry on and tell the story, and the words in this book will help to keep the story alive for generations to come.

Hers was a life of good energy and love that were unequaled; they were lessons for me in life, a dogma and teaching. They will do that for my family, for the many people who knew her in life, and for those who read these words. It was a short life lived, but hopefully will be cherished even more after life.

Afterword

If you have lived, you have suffered. You have grieved. You have loved. You have lost. It is the inevitable debt of which we pay in exchange for life.

These emotions we have all experienced are a quintessential part of the human experience. It is only in the acceptance of the pain, sorrow and hurt, which we must surrender, that we can continue. Surrender to a greater will in the heavens, while having the knowledge and conviction that out of it all, life, love and hope reemerge. Feelings that, for a few moments, you believe had died.

Different people experience grief differently, but we all share certain aspects. Out of loss comes grief and sadness, and dismay and disbelief follow not far behind. Anger takes hold of all your senses: anger at people, anger at God, anger at yourself. There may follow a strong desire for isolation. Some bad habits might take hold, such as excessive drinking, smoking, or the use of mind-altering substances. Anything to allow escape. But time is what is needed. Time is the answer. I used to hear, and now believe it wholeheartedly, that distance in time and space allows for a quicker recovery. Understanding each phase while we are grieving is key to put things in a positive and constructive perspective.

As one guru said, "I realize that they are there: suffering, death, grief, etc. I stop, acknowledge; I pay no mind anymore; I accept and move on." I have frequently asked myself, why am I going through this? There must be a reason. There has to be a lesson here. I ask the almighty, "Please show me and guide me to what I need to learn from this." The almighty replies, *"And ye dislike it. But it is possible that ye dislike a thing which is good for you, and that ye love a thing which is bad for you. But Allah knoweth, and ye know not."*

I have no doubt in my mind that a manifestation will appear and the answers will become clear. So I accept the test from above, and surrender to the greater will, for salvation is in the end and a positive outcome is always the final result. God is great indeed.

I hope that you, the reader, can see through my eyes and realize that, in fact, as humans we are all equal, and it is the same when it comes to feelings associated with grief and suffering for lost ones. It is an amazing fact that as a Muslim, I found greater commonality with others from all major faiths as I walked through my experience. The love my Muslim brethren showed me was no greater or less than that offered by other Christians, Jews, and even non-religious people.

I walked away from this, and if you take nothing from my book please take this knowledge that I wish someone had given me in the beginning, the conviction that we as humans are one. We share that common seed from the one and only creator that we may refer to in different words and with different dogmas. Coexistence between all these faiths should be natural and ought not to even be a discussion, for we are all the same and coexisting in essence with each other!

In the end it all works out if we keep holding on to what is center and focus.

Amen.

In Said Nedlouf's memoir, *Rage and Resilience: A Journey through My Beloved's Battle with Cancer,* the author tugs at your heartstrings while recounting the struggle and battle his beloved late wife, Mary Kathryn endured during her battle with cancer. After a time together of over two decades, Nedlouf eloquently expresses how he endured the three stages of grief: denial, anger, and with a strong faith, finally acceptance. Nedlouf proves how two different cultures can coexist. Nedlouf, being a devout member of the Islamic faith, fell in love with a Christian Catholic, Mary Kathryn, also called MK. This heartwarming love story proves that people of different faiths and cultures can coexist and create their own fairytale love story. After reading Said Nedlouf's memoir, you too can find yourself wearing a blindfold and only seeing people for the beautiful soul that resides within them.

Printed in the United States
By Bookmasters